Pure Labrador Cookbook

Featuring Pure Labrador Preserves
&
Traditional Recipes from Labrador

Compiled by
The Coastal Heritage Project and
Pure Labrador Preserves

ISBN: 978-1-895109-66-5

Published by
James Lane Publishing
43 James Lane
St. John's, NL, Canada
A1E 3H3
Tel: 1-888-588-6353
Fax: 1-709-726-2135
Website: www.jameslanepublishing.com
Email: mail@jameslanepublishing.com

Printed by Friesens Corporation in Altona, MB, Canada

Pure Labrador Cookbook

About the Cookbook

This cookbook contains heritage recipes and stories from the Labrador Straits collected by a community project, the Coastal Heritage Experience. We have partnered with Pure Labrador Preserves, a local company owned and operated by the Flynn family of Forteau, Labrador, to include contemporary berry recipes using their products and recipes from their family restaurant. These recipes have been written by Ethel Flynn, who has cooked in the restaurant for many years and is about to retire. Ethel and her sister Nancy have also shared some family memories with us. The introduction has been written by a close friend of the Flynn family, Lynn Palmer.

We would like to thank the 170 individuals who shared their memories with us throughout the project, and in particular those whose stories and recipes are included in this cookbook. We would also like to thank our project partners: SmartLabrador, the Labrador Straits Historical Development Corporation, the Labrador Straits Development Corporation, Parks Canada, the Atlantic Canada Opportunities Agency, and the Department of Industry Trade and Rural Development.

The Coastal Heritage Project Team

Pure Labrador Cookbook

Introduction

Naturally I was honoured when Stelman asked me to write the introduction to the *Pure Labrador Cookbook*. When I was a child, Labrador was a place often spoken of by my parents, their siblings and their friends in stories replete with nostalgia, fond memories and a longing to return. To me, the word Labrador was synonymous with bakeapples - pure gold at the best of times. Our cache arrived magically in two cases of quart sized mason jars each fall and were meted out judiciously throughout the year until the next shipment came.

My family roots go deep into the beaches, the barrens and the berry patches; up the Forteau and the Pinware Rivers; out the old "roads" to Point Amour, Fox Cove and Buckle's Point, along Whistle House Brook, and around the Battery. There is a generational link between Stelman and I.

In 1922 my maternal grandfather was appointed the Senior Wireless Operator at Point Amour. My grandmother, Mary Jane (Mercer) Barrett had a best friend, Aunt Mary Barney from nearby Fox Cove and my mother's best friend was her daughter, Isabella Lily Barney (Bella) who later married Wilfred George Flynn (Wiff) and they became the parents of Stelman, Ethel, Maggie and Nancy.

My first visit to Labrador was in 1975 when my dad's sister, Maud (Palmer) Belbin; my sister, Verda Russell and her baby daughter, Kerri; and I piled into my little Volkswagen bug and set off on our magic carpet ride across Newfoundland from the Avalon Peninsula, up the Northern Peninsula and caught the ferry across the Strait of Belle Isle to Blanc Sablon. The first beach we saw at L'Anse au Clair left us breathless - a sensation that remained with us throughout our ten day visit. Aunt Maud made the introductions and people whose names we'd heard spoken became real to us. We were treated like royalty and then regaled with the nostalgic Labrador versions of the stories we'd heard at home.   All these extended family members and family friends now became real for us as we were now able to live our family history - very significant to me as, under one roof in Forteau, we had four generations: my paternal grandmother's sister, Aunt Mame (Buckle) Davis, Aunt Maud, Verda and I, and Kerri - who took her very first steps there in Forteau.

Into this mix came the turning point for "our" generation because this is when we met Stelman; our cousin, Hazel Roberts; Nita Hancock; and Rev. Martin Lane. Laughter ruled the days and nights when the six of us were together - especially as we watched this foursome perform in a "time" in the gymnasium of the high school. My friendship with Stelman evolved from this visit.

It's important to note that in subsequent years since 1975, I've been so fortunate to have made many pilgrimages back to The Straits - on my own, with my parents and with my husband, Larry Stephan.

From the moment I catch my first glimpse of the Point Amour Lighthouse from the Newfoundland side until the wheels hit the pavement in Blanc Sablon the emotional momentum builds. It grows until I come down the road into Forteau and it continues until I've retraced those steps: on the beaches and on the barrens; seen the berry patches, the Battery and the Pinware River; walked from L'Anse Amour out the old "roads" to Point Amour, sat in the seat in the rocks where my parents courted, dipped my fingers in Whistle House Brook; been to Fox Cove and Buckle's Point; and thanks to Hollis Buckle I've now seen Uncle Henry's Rock on the Forteau River.

Nancy Flynn in Aunt Bella's Bakery

How appropriate it is that from Ethel's kitchen where the old wood stove is juxtaposed with the modern electric stove many of the recipes within these covers have been developed, tested and fine tuned. The love and pride of family shared amongst Ethel, Maggie, Nancy, Stelman and their siblings; the work ethic they all practice and the spirit of entrepreneurship they embrace comes to them honestly.

It's been handed down from their grandmother, Aunt Mary Barney who moved from Forteau to Fox Cove. Living there, she'd have better access to the beach and would be able to wheel their grandfather, Uncle Will, who was severely crippled, in a wheelbarrow to his boat so that he could fish each day.

Ethel Flynn in Aunt Bella's Bakery

Aunt Mary passed these qualities directly on to Aunt Bella who worked alongside Wiff to run his shop, while at the same time Bella cooked and cleaned house and baked for her family long before she had the luxury of an automatic washer or an electric mixer. From the start of his business venture, she worked with Stelman hand peeling and slicing all the potatoes to make french fries, making and baking hot dog buns and hamburger buns, making gravies, doing the laundry from the restaurant - helping out whenever and wherever she could. Throughout her lifetime, she never turned a blind eye to the needs of others.

Without the luxury of supermarkets and specialty stores, past generations stretched the supplies in the larder and worked with fish, game, berries, and - if they were fortunate - supplemented these with fresh vegetables from their home gardens in order to provide the most nutritious and filling meals for their families that they could. Surely their daily mantra was: "whatever needs doing, just get it done in the best way possible but always to the best of your ability".

The *Pure Labrador Cookbook* is a most fitting tribute to Aunt Mary, Aunt Bella, Ethel, Maggie and Nancy - a tangible homage to them and the many other unbelievably strong women who have been and continue to represent our heritage and to be role models for all of us.

Lynn Palmer
June 14, 2010

House & Garden
Table of Contents

Land & Sea
Table of Contents

Land & Sea
Table of Contents

Bread & Buns
Table of Contents

Holidays & Times
Table of Contents

Orange and Red Onion Salad with Lingonberry (Partridgeberry) Vinaigrette

	Mixed baby salad greens	
4	large seedless oranges	4
1	pink grapefruit	1
1	small red onion, very thinly sliced	1
2 tbsp	coarsely chopped fresh mint	30 ml

1. Place bed of greens on four plates.

2. Cut off ends of the oranges and grapefruit revealing the flesh. Stand each orange on a cutting surface and with a sharp knife, slice off the peel making sure to remove all the peel and white membrane. Repeat the same procedure with the grapefruit. Slice the oranges and the grapefruit, removing all seeds. Lay slices of orange and grapefruit on the greens.

3. Lay concentric rings of red onions over the fruit. Sprinkle with mint.

4. Drizzle the salads with the Lingonberry (Partridgeberry) Vinaigrette. Serves 4.

Lingonberry (Partridgeberry) Vinaigrette

3 tbsp	Pure Labrador Lingonberry (Partridgeberry) Syrup	45 ml
1 tbsp	red wine vinegar	15 ml
3 tbsp	olive oil	45 ml
	Salt and pepper to taste	

1. Combine all ingredients and whisk until well blended

Mixed Greens, Carrots, and Fruit Salad

1	orange	1
1	pear or apple	1
2	carrots, peeled and grated	2
½ cup	thinly sliced red onion	125 ml
4 cups	mixed greens	1 litre
2 cups	arugula leaves	500 ml
½ tsp	coarse sea salt	2 ml

1. Peel the orange removing all the white membrane. Cut into sections.

2. Quarter the pear and slice thinly.

3. Place greens in large bowl and toss with 5 Tbsp (75 ml) dressing. Divide onto 4 plates.

4. Sprinkle carrots over lettuce. Arrange oranges and pear slices attractively over top.

5. Garnish with onion slices and a sprinkling of sea salt.

6. Serve with Pure Labrador Cloudberry (Bakeapple) Dressing

Cloudberry (Bakeapple) Dressing

4 tbsp	olive oil	60 ml
2 tbsp	white wine vinegar	30 ml
4 tbsp	Pure Labrador Cloudberry (Bakeapple) Syrup	60 ml
½ tsp	Dijon mustard	2 ml
1/8 tsp	black pepper	.5 ml

1. Whisk all ingredients together. Refrigerate until ready to use.

Cloudberry (Bakeapple) Glazed Tofu

1 lb	extra firm tofu	454 g
2 tbsp	olive oil	30 ml
3 tbsp	Pure Labrador Cloudberry (Bakeapple) Syrup	45 ml
2 tbsp	tamari or soy sauce	30 ml

1. Cut tofu into ¼ inch slices. Blot between several layers of paper towels.

2. Slowly heat the olive oil, Cloudberry Syrup and tamari in a large frying pan.

3. Add the slices of tofu, turning them quickly to coat both sides. Sauté over medium-high heat until golden brown and crisp on both sides, about 10 minutes.   Serves 4.

Thai Salad Dressing

1/3 cup	peanut butter	80 ml
1 cup	boiling water	250 ml
¼ cup	granulated white sugar or honey	60 ml
1 tsp	salt	5 ml
3 cloves	garlic minced	3
	crushed red pepper or cayenne to taste	
2 tsp	fresh lime or lemon juice	10 ml

In a small bowl whisk peanut butter and boiling water until well blended. Stir in remaining ingredients.

Partridgeberry Cottage Cheese Salad
(Excellent served with fish)

1 envelope	unflavored gelatin	1
¼ cup	cold water	60 ml
2 cups	Pure Labrador Lingonberry (Partridgeberry) Spread	500 ml
2 tsp	horseradish	10 ml
¾ tsp	dry mustard	3 ml
1 tsp	freshly grated lemon peel	5 ml
¼ cup	lemon juice	60 ml
¼ tsp	salt	1 ml
Pinch	cayenne	Pinch
¾ cup	cottage cheese	185 ml

1. Place gelatin in custard cup. Add cold water. Let stand 2 minutes.
2. Place custard cup in pan of boiling water until gelatin dissolves.
3. Combine Pure Labrador Lingonberry (Partridgeberry) Spread and gelatin. Stir in other ingredients heating slightly to blend.
4. Spoon into mould, which has been rinsed in cold water. Chill until firm.
5. Remove mould and serve in lettuce cups.

Apple Cottage Cheese Salad

2	Granny Smith apples diced	2
1 cup	cottage cheese	250 ml
1 cup	green cabbage, shredded	250 ml
3 tbsp	roasted sunflower seeds	45 ml
3 tbsp	chopped pecans toasted	45 ml
2 tbsp	light mayonnaise	30 ml
¼ tsp	pepper	1 ml

1. Put ingredients in a large bowl and toss gently.

Menu for a Week
As told to us by Ruby Cabot.

Usually in the early years when we were growing up, back in the 30's and 40's, they use to try and do up their menus as best they could for their weekly meals.

On Sundays, mostly every Sunday, we'd have fish and brewis for breakfast, coffee or tea. Then for dinner, we'd have, well if you had rabbit, you'd have a baked rabbit, or some sea birds or it'd be birds, not very often we'd have any meat. But anyway, we'd either have birds or rabbit with vegetables, and pudding and tea, that would be for dinner. For supper, we would have the bread, cake and some cheese maybe, prunes or jelly and custard and tea. That would be our Sunday menu.

Monday for breakfast would be roast capelin, jam bread and tea. Dinner, it would be boiled beans, or hash and the hash would be made from the vegetables left from the Sunday dinner, and tea. For supper we would have soup. Mom use to always make, what you calls a butter soup. What she would do to make a butter soup was she'd put some butter in the boiler and some onions, fry the onions and throw the water in on that, put the vegetables, and the can of tomato stuff in, and the rice and that would be her soup. So we'd have soup with dumplings and tea and molasses or molasses cake or whatever we had.

On Tuesday, we'd have porridge and toast and 'fer dinner we would have a jigs dinner with dumplings, spread with jam and tea. And for supper we'd have hash made from the vegetables left from dinner and we'd have some vinegar pie.

In order to make a vinegar pie, you get a cup of vinegar, 1 and ½ cups of water, ½ cup of sugar, and ½ teaspoon of spice. You boil all that together for 10 minutes, and then you thicken it with a corn starch, and you make it or with an ordinary flour. You make a thick paste, and then you fill the paste, fill the shell with this filling and you bake at 400 degrees until nice and brown and that's a nice vinegar pie.

Old Fashioned Potato Soup

6	potatoes, peeled and diced	6
6	onions, sliced thinly	6
6	stalks celery, chopped	6
4 cups	boiling water	1 L
2 tbsp	butter	30 ml
2 tbsp	all purpose flour	30 ml
4 cups	milk scalded	1 L
	Salt and pepper to taste	
6 slices	bacon (fried crisp and crumbled)	6
	Paprika, parsley & chives to garnish	

1. Cover potatoes, onion and celery with boiling water. Boil until soft. Remove vegetables but retain the water.
2. Force vegetables through sieve or puree in food processor or blender.
3. Make white sauce in a small heavy saucepan over moderate heat: melt butter, whisk in flour and the water retained from cooking the vegetables. Stir constantly until thickened and smooth, about 3 minutes.
4. Stir in mashed vegetables. Add milk, salt and pepper to taste. Stir frequently and heat slowly. <u>Do not boil.</u>
5. Just before serving, stir in crumbled bacon.
6. Garnish each individual portion with paprika, parsley and chives and float a little butter on top.

Home Remedies

Cora Barney shares some home remedies used over the years by older people.

If you got a cut on your hand, or on your wrist or anywhere, you use turpentine and it seals the cut and it prevents infection from getting in. And you get turpentine from the trees, here in the back woods. You go out there. Often my brothers would go out and cut off a piece of turpentine and bring it home and ah we'd use it for cuts and different things, you know.*

And if you're out on the ski-doo in the winter time and you get snow blind, when you come home, slice some raw potato, lie down and put the potatoes on your eyes - for as long as it takes, I guess.

If you got a real sore throat from mumps, drink some cod liver oil, it really soothes the throat. It tastes awful, but it works.

Also mustard plaster, if you got problems with your chest, you must have heard of this one before - mustard plaster, you mix up the dry mustard according to the direction on the box, you spread it on a flannel it has to be flannel, not cotton, and apply it to the chest area. It helps to draw out the infection.

If you got a toothache, and I remember mom doing this, I mean, I must have looked crazy, going around with a thing wrapped around my head. She use to slice raw potato and put it in a flannel and wrapped it around my neck, around my head or wherever the toothache was. I still remember me going around with this thing tied around my head and it worked, or maybe there again, it's all in the head, but that was one we did use and it was fine.

**Turpentine is the sap from a fir tree.*

Curried Salt Cod Salad

1 lb	salt cod	454 g
1 tbsp	fresh lemon juice	15 ml
1	red apple, unpeeled and diced	1
1 cup	celery, diced with leaves	250 ml
	Romaine lettuce	
½ cup	raisins	125 ml
½ cup	chopped onions	125 ml
½ cup	Pure Labrador Lingonberry (Partridgeberry) Vinaigrette	125 ml

1. Soak fish overnight and parboil for 10 minutes.
2. Remove from heat, discard all skin and bones.
3. Flake fish into bite sized pieces and chill.
4. Sprinkle lemon juice over diced apple to prevent discolouration.
5. Combine apple, celery, raisins and onion. Add fish.
6. Mix curry powder with dressing. Combine with fish mixture and toss lightly.
7. Serve on bed of lettuce.

Lingonberry (Partridgeberry) Vinaigrette

3 tbsp	Pure Labrador Lingonberry (Partridgeberry) Syrup	45 ml
1 tbsp	red wine vinegar	15 ml
3 tbsp	olive oil	45 ml
	Salt and pepper	

1. Combine all ingredients and whisk until well blended.

Beet Coleslaw

Dill Dressing:

½ cup	light mayonnaise	125 ml
1 tbsp	lemon juice	15 ml
½ tsp	dried dill	2 ml
½ tsp	dry mustard	2 ml

1. Combine all ingredients in small bowl, set aside

Coleslaw:

2 cups	green cabbage, shredded	500 ml
1 cup	red cabbage, shredded	250 ml
2 cups	cooked beets, diced	500 ml
1 cup	cottage cheese	250 ml

1. Put all ingredients in a bowl. Toss well with dressing.

Cauliflower and Lettuce Salad

½	Romaine lettuce	1/2
½	cauliflower	1/2
4	hard-boiled eggs, diced	4
¼ lb	cheddar cheese, grated	113 g
¼ lb	bacon	113 g

1. Combine lettuce, cauliflower, eggs and cheese. Toss with dressing.

Dressing:

1 ½ cup	mayonnaise	375 ml
1/3 cup	parmesan cheese	80 ml
¼ cup	granulated white sugar	60 ml

1. Mix together mayonnaise, parmesan cheese and sugar.
2. Toss dressing with salad.
3. Fry, drain and crumble bacon. Sprinkle over salad and serve.

Pea Soup

1 lb	salt beef or ham bone	454 g
1 pkg	split peas	
8 cups	cold water	2 L
3 cup	turnip diced	750 ml
3 cup	carrots diced	750 ml
1	large onion chopped	1
1 tsp	pepper	5 ml

1. If using salt beef, cut in small pieces, cover with water and boil for 15 to 20 minutes then drain meat, saving the water to add to the soup (if necessary) instead of adding salt Set aside.
2. Put 8 cups of cold water in a large pot, add split peas. Bring to boil. Add salt beef or ham bone return to boil, reduce heat and simmer for 1 ½ hours.
3. Add vegetables and cook for another 40 minutes.
4. Add dumplings.

Dumplings:

2 cups	all purpose flour	500 ml
1 tbsp	butter or vegetable oil	15 ml
4 tsp	baking powder	20 ml
¾ cup	cold water or milk	185 ml

Mix together flour, butter, and baking powder, add water to make a soft dough. Drop by tablespoons in soup. Cover and bring to boil. <u>Do not remove lid.</u> Reduce heat and simmer for 10 minutes.

Broccoli, Cauliflower and Pea Salad

2 cups	broccoli florets	500 ml
2 cups	cauliflower florets	500 ml
2 cups	frozen green peas thawed	500 ml
1	large onion, chopped	1
2 cups	celery, chopped	500 ml
¾ cup	sour cream	185 ml
¾ cup	mayonnaise	185 ml
2 tbsp	granulated white sugar	30 ml
2 tbsp	vinegar	30 ml
¼ tsp	salt	1 ml

1. Combine all ingredients.
2. Refrigerate overnight and serve.

Variation:
Add one can sliced water chestnuts.

Butternut Squash Soup

1	medium onion, chopped	1
2	cloves garlic, chopped	2
1	medium squash, cubed	1
4	carrots, diced	4
2	large potatoes, diced	2
1 tbsp	fresh gingerroot, peeled and chopped	15 ml
3 ½ cups	chicken broth	900 ml
	salt and pepper to taste	

1. In medium saucepan, sauté onions and garlic in oil until tender.
2. Add chicken broth to remaining ingredients.
3. Cover and simmer for 30 minutes or until vegetables are soft.
4. Remove from heat and process in small batches in a blender, until smooth.
5. Return to saucepan and heat slowly to desired serving temperature. At serving, garnish with a dollop of sour cream and drag toothpick through the cream to make the desired pattern.

Chinese Cabbage Salad

Dressing:

¼ cup	white vinegar	60 ml
¼ cup	granulated white sugar	60 ml
1 ½ tbsp	soy sauce	22 ml
¼ tsp	sesame oil	1 ml
¼ cup	olive oil	60 ml

1. Whisk all ingredients until well blended.
2. Put in small saucepan and bring to boil.
3. Boil for 2 minutes, remove from heat and cool.

Salad:

½	Chinese cabbage, sliced finely	½
½	red pepper diced	½
3	green onions sliced	3
¼ cup	almonds, toasted	60 ml
2 tsp	sesame seeds, toasted	10 ml

1. Combine salad ingredients.
2. Add dressing.

To Serve:

| 1 pkg | Mr. Noodles crumbled | 1 |

1. Just before serving, sprinkle noodles over salad.

Moose Soup

2 lb	moose	1 kg
1 lb	salt beef	454g
32 cups	water	4 L
3 or 4	carrots, chopped	3 or 4
2 stalks	celery, chopped	2
2	onions, diced	2
1	medium turnip, chopped	1
½ cup	Minute Rice	250 ml

1. Cut moose meat and salt beef in small pieces.
2. Add to water in stockpot and simmer for two hours.
3. Add vegetables and cook for 45 minutes.
4. Then add rice and cook for another 20 minutes.

Rabbit Soup

1 tbsp	olive oil	15 ml
1	rabbit, cleaned and cut in small pieces	1
14 cups	water	3.5 L
1 lb	salt beef, fat removed and cut in small pieces	454 g
½ tsp	pepper	2 ml
1	small turnip, chopped	1
3 or 4	carrots, chopped	3 or 4
2	onions, chopped	2
½ cup	Minute Rice	125 ml

1. Fry rabbit in olive oil for 20 minutes.
2. Add water and salt beef and boil for 1 ½ hour.
3. Add vegetables and cook for an additional 45 minutes.
4. Add rice and cook for a further 20 to 25 minutes.

Navy Bean Soup

2 cups	navy beans	500 ml
10 cups	water	2.5 L
1	large onion, chopped	1
2	stalks celery, chopped	2
1	small turnip, chopped	1
2	carrots	2
2	cloves garlic	2
1 can	14oz tomatoes	398 ml
	salt and pepper to taste	
1	bay leaf	1

1. Put beans and water in large pot, simmer until tender 45 minutes to 1 hour. Add remaining ingredients and cook until vegetables are tender, 1 ½ to 2 hours

Corn Chowder

5 slices	bacon	5
1	medium onion, chopped	1
1 cup	celery, chopped	250 ml
2	large potatoes (peeled and cubed)	2
4 cups	milk	1 L
¾ cup	kernel corn	185 ml
1 tsp	salt	5 ml
½ tsp	freshly ground pepper	2 ml
½ tsp	Tabasco sauce	2 ml

1. Fry the bacon in a large saucepan, just until it begins to brown.
2. Add onions, celery and potato.
3. Cook over medium heat stirring occasionally until onions are soft.
4. Add the remaining ingredients. Cover and heat, but do not boil.
5. Reduce heat and simmer for 20 to 25 minutes or until potatoes are tender. Stir often.

Old Fashioned Cabbage Hash
A heritage recipe as told to us by Myrtle Jones.

You take one green cabbage from your garden, fresh from your garden, medium head of cabbage, mostly with green, first when they're growing up. And a nice few new potatoes, like probably, half a dozen probably ten or twelve if they're small, you know. And you cut up your cabbage, wash your cabbage and cut it up, and you scrape your potatoes and you cut them up and you fry out pork slices. Just four or five slices of pork.

You add the onion and the chopped cabbage with enough water to cover, barely cover until the cabbage and the onion is nearly done. Then you add your potatoes, you cut up potatoes and a bit of pepper and salt and you cook until done.

Then, to make it better, you puts a slice of homemade bread in your plate and covers with the cabbage hash. And it's really good.

Poached Eggs with Ham and Veggie Hash

2 tsp	vegetable oil	10 ml
¼ lb	smoked ham	113 g
1	potato peeled and diced	1
1	small onion	1
¼ cup	chicken or vegetable stock	60 ml
¼ tsp	hot pepper sauce	1 ml
½	green pepper, diced	1/2
½ cup	corn kernels	125 ml
1	small tomato (diced)	1
2	eggs	2
	parsley to garnish	

1. In 7 inch skillet, heat oil over medium heat.
2. Add ham, potato, and onion, stirring often and cook for three minutes.
3. Add stock and hot sauce. Cover and cook over medium heat until potatoes are almost tender.
4. Add green pepper, corn and tomato.
5. Make two nests in mixture, crack one egg into each nest.
6. Cook covered for five minutes or until eggs are set.
7. Garnish with parsley and serve

Roasted Winter Vegetables with Cloudberry (Bakeapple) Glaze

4	parsnips	4
2	large carrots	2
2	small sweet potatoes	2
4	beets	4
8	cloves garlic, peeled	8
¼ cup	olive oil	60 ml
¼ cup	Pure Labrador Cloudberry (Bakeapple) Syrup	60 ml
1 tsp	cumin seed	5 ml
½ tsp	black pepper	2 ml
½ tsp	salt	2 ml

1. Preheat oven 400° F.

2. Scrub the vegetables, cutting off any bad spots. Cut in 4 inch lengths. Cut the sweet potatoes, beets and carrots in wedges. Place in large bowl.

3. Mix together the rest of the ingredients. Pour over the vegetables. Stir together until the vegetables are coated. Spread in single layer in baking pan. Scrape any glaze remaining in bowl over the vegetables.

4. Bake in oven 40 to 50 minutes, tossing once, until browned on the outside and tender inside.   Serves: 4

Vegetables Supreme

Preheat oven to 350° F.

2 cup	broccoli, chopped	500 ml
2 cups	cauliflower, chopped	500 ml
2	eggs, well beaten	2
½ cup	mayonnaise	125 ml
1	medium onion, chopped	1
1 cup	cream of mushroom soup	250 ml
1 cup	grated cheese	250 ml
1 box	seasoned croutons, crushed	1
¼ cup	butter, melted	60 ml

1. Cook broccoli and cauliflower for 4 to 5 minutes, drain. Place in 8" x 8" casserole dish
2. Beat eggs.
3. Combine eggs, mayonnaise, onion, soup, and ½ cup grated cheese.
4. Pour over vegetables. Sprinkle with remaining cheese.
5. Toss crushed croutons with melted butter and sprinkle over top of casserole.
6. Bake at 350° F for 40 minutes or until lightly browned

Turnip au Gratin

1 tsp	sugar	5 ml
2 cups	water	500 ml
2 lb	turnip	1 kg
1	onion chopped	1
2	eggs	2
2 tsp	butter, melted	10 ml
½ tsp	salt	2 ml
Pinch	pepper	Pinch
¼ tsp	paprika	1 ml
½ cup	fine breadcrumbs	125 ml
½ cup	grated cheddar cheese	125 ml

1. Dissolve sugar in water in medium saucepan.
2. Add turnip and cook until tender.
3. Drain and mash.
4. Beat well eggs, butter, salt, pepper and paprika
5. Mix with turnip. Blend well.
6. Put in 2 quart casserole dish.
7. Sprinkle with cheese and breadcrumbs. Bake uncovered in 350° F oven for 30 minutes.

Old Fashioned Home Remedies
Anonymous

If you are in a tent, or cabin, and the flies are about to eat you alive, put a handful of blackberry bush on the fire and let some of the smoke into the tent. Your eyes may sting a little, but the flies will disappear. If you are outside and can't get in out of the flies, smear on mud. Cover your hands, face, and any exposed area. The grey, sticky stuff is best.

For all ailments, including loss of appetite, dirty blood and lack of vitamins, peel the bark from the black spruce tree, cut into pieces and place in a pot of water. Bring to a boil. Let simmer for an hour. Remove from heat and let cool. Store in jars and drink a glass each day as a tonic.

When cod liver is fried, mix with a few berries and eat as a source of vitamins.

To help heal bruises quickly, cut a thin strip of seal fat from the seal. Wrap it in a clean cloth and tie it securely around the bruised area. Change frequently. Do not use this method if you have any broken skin along with the bruise.

For colds, mix together equal amounts of molasses and vinegar. Take one teaspoon, as needed. If you are plagued with colds often, eat rabbit soup once in a while. The vitamins will boost your metabolism and the hot soup will make you feel better.

For diaper rash, brown flour. Place a cup of regular, white, flour in the bottom of a pan. Place the pan on the stove. Make sure the stove is not too hot or the flour will burn. Stir continuously until the flour is golden brown. Remove from heat. Cool and mix well. Pour into a shaker and sprinkle on baby's bottom at each diaper change.

For an earache, take a flat rock and warm it in the oven. Wrap in a towel and place over the ear. The heat helps relieve pain. A plate, or a flatiron can be used in the same manner.

For respiratory problems, bake a goose for dinner! After the bird is cooked drain the grease into a jar. Cool. The grease becomes thick when cooled. Take a good dollop and rub on the back and chest.

Cloudberry (Bakeapple) Infused Salmon with Potato Crisps

Yield: 4 servings
48oz   salmon fillets, skinned and boneless   1.25 kg
½ cup   Pure Labrador Cloudberry (Bakeapple) Marinade   125 ml

1. Marinate the salmon fillets in the marinade for 24 hours.
2. Remove the fillets from marinade and place on a lightly greased baking sheet. Brush any remaining marinade over the fillets.
3. Bake at 375° for 10 to 20 minutes depending on thickness. Check for doneness by inserting a knife and checking if it is cooked.
4. Place on a potato crisp and serve.

Pure Labrador Cloudberry (Bakeapple) Marinade

6 tbsp   Pure Labrador Cloudberry (Bakeapple) Syrup   90 ml
2 tsp   gingerroot, peeled and finely grated   10 ml
4 tsp   fresh lemon juice   20 ml
1 tbsp   soy sauce   15 ml
1 clove   garlic, minced   1
Salt and pepper to taste

1. Blend all ingredients together. Yield: ½ cup (125 ml)

Potato Crisps

(May be prepared ahead of time and reheated to serve.)

2 lb	potatoes	1 kg
½ cup	onions, minced	125 ml
¼ cup	all-purpose flour	60 ml
1 tbsp	baking powder	15 ml
½ tsp	salt	2 ml
¼ tsp	each black pepper and nutmeg	1 ml
2	beaten eggs	2
¼ cup	vegetable oil for frying	60 ml

1. Peel and grate potatoes.

2. Mix together the onions and potatoes.

3. Mix together the flour, baking powder, salt, pepper and nutmeg. Stir into the potato/onion mixture. Add the beaten egg and mix well.

4. Heat frying pan over medium heat. Add 1 tbsp (15 ml) vegetable oil. Drop heaping spoonfuls of potato mixture onto hot pan and flatten with back of spoon. Fry 1 2 minutes per side until browned.

5. Remove potato crisps to paper towel to drain. Add more oil to pan and continue frying crisps until all the batter is cooked.

6. Reheat when ready to serve. Yield: 16 14 3-inch crisps

Scallop Mornay

Preheat oven to 350° F.

1	onion	1

Bouquet Garni:

	Bay leaf, parsley and thyme	
	1 to 2 cups white wine	500 ml
	Salt and Pepper	
¼ cup	butter	60 ml
¼ cup	all purpose flour	60 ml
1 cup	cream	250 ml
2 lbs	scallops cut in half	1 kg
½ cup	bread crumbs	125 ml
½ cup	cheese, grated	227 g

1. Combine onion bouquet garni, salt and pepper in sauce pan and white wine. Gently bring to a boil and simmer for two minutes.
2. Drain and reserve stock.
3. In separate pan melt butter, add flour, and cook for two minutes.
4. Slowly add cream, stirring constantly.
5. Add stock and scallops. Bring to a boil. Remove from heat immediately
6. Pour into greased casserole dish and top with bread crumbs and cheese.
7. Bake at 350° F, approximately 10 minutes or until cheese is melted.

Scallops Supreme

White Sauce:

4 tbsp	butter	60 ml
4 tbsp	all purpose flour	60 ml
1 tsp	salt	5 ml
2 cups	milk	500 ml
½ tsp	pepper	2 ml

1. In a saucepan, melt butter for sauce. Blend in flour, salt, and pepper.
2. Gradually add milk. Stir until smooth. Bring to boil. Preheat oven to 350 degrees.

½ lb	mushrooms sliced	227 g
1	medium onion chopped fine	1
2 tbsp	butter	60 ml
1lb	scallops	454 g
1 cup	bread crumbs	250 ml
1 cup	cheddar cheese, grated	250 ml
3 cups	cooked eggs noodles (wide)	750 ml

1. Sauté mushrooms and onions in butter for 10 minutes
2. Add scallops and noodles to the sauce with mushrooms and onions.
3. Sprinkle with breadcrumbs and cheese. Bake at 350° F for 25 minutes.

Broccoli and Scallops

8 cups	water	2L
1 tsp	salt	5 ml
3 cups	macaroni	750 ml
3 cups	broccoli	750 ml
1 tbsp	butter	15 ml
4 tsp	flour	20 ml
1 ½ cups	chicken or vegetable broth	375 ml
½ cup	herb and garlic spreadable cream cheese	125 ml
1 lb	scallops	454 g

1. Combine water and salt in large saucepan, bring to a boil. Add pasta and boil uncovered for eight minutes, stirring occasionally. Add broccoli and cook uncovered for two to four minutes, stirring occasionally until pasta is tender but firm and broccoli is tender crisp. Drain. Return to pot and cover to keep warm.
2. Heat butter in separate saucepan on medium. Add flour. Heat and stir for one minute. Add broth, whisking constantly until smooth. Add cream cheese. Whisk until smooth.
3. Add scallops and pasta mixture.
4. Cook for 2 to 4 minutes and serve.

Amazing Crab Cakes

2	eggs	2
2 cups	cooked rice	500 ml
2 cans (12 oz each)	crabmeat, well drained	350 g
¼ cup	grated Parmesan cheese	60 ml
¼ cup	margarine, melted	60 ml

1. Beat eggs well.
2. Add rice, crab and cheese. Mix together well.
3. Divide into 8 patties. Let stand 5 minutes.
4. Heat oil in heavy frying pan and fry patties 5 minutes per side.

Codfish Cakes

A heritage recipe as told to us by Marie Marshall

1 med. onion chopped fine
2 cups cooked salt codfish, boned and shredded
6-8 cooked potatoes
¼ tsp. pepper
1 tsp. savory

Mash potatoes and add remaining ingredients. Form into cakes, roll in flour and fry in rendered pork fat. (Salmon may be used in place of salt codfish.)

Seafood Chowder

½ cup	butter	113 g
3 to 4	potatoes diced	3 to 4
2 stalks	celery diced	2
2	carrots diced	2
1	large onion diced	1
1	clove garlic minced	1
½ cup	flour	125 ml
8 cups	fish stock	2 litres
½ lb	salmon cubed	227 g
½ lb	cod fish	227 g
1	medium halibut fillet	1
¼ lb	sea scallops, cut in half	113 g
½ cup	whipping cream	125 ml
½ tsp	pepper	2 ml
4 tsp	fresh dill, chopped	20 ml
	Salt to taste	

1. In large heavy saucepan, melt butter over medium heat.
2. Add potatoes, celery, carrots, onion and garlic and cook for 8 minutes, or until softened.
3. Blend in flour.
4. Reserve 1 cup of stock (250ml) and gradually whisk in remaining stock, stirring constantly. Bring to boil.
5. Reduce heat and simmer, covered for about 10 minutes or until vegetables are tender.
6. Meanwhile, in a separate saucepan bring reserved cup of stock (250 ml) to a boil. Reduce heat to simmer and poach salmon, cod and halibut for two minutes.
7. Remove with slotted spoon and set aside. Keep warm.
8. Poach scallops for one minute. Add salmon, cod, halibut and scallops to vegetable mixture.
9. Gradually add cream, dill, pepper and salt to taste.
10. Heat slowly. Do not boil.

Scallop Casserole

Preheat oven to 375° F.

1 cup	cooked rice	250 ml
2 tbsp	oil	30 ml
1	large onion	1
1	green pepper	1
1 cup	mushrooms sliced	250 ml
	Salt and pepper to taste	
1 cup	frozen peas or mixed vegetables	250 ml
1 lb	scallops (uncooked)	454 g
½ cup	bread crumbs	125 ml
2 tbsp	butter, melted	30 ml

1. Wash scallops, pat dry and set aside.
2. Sauté onions, green pepper and mushrooms in oil. Season with salt and pepper
3. Put cooked rice in the bottom of a casserole dish. Cover with sautéed onions, green pepper and mushrooms. Add frozen peas or mixed vegetables.
4. Add scallops.
5. Spread with cheese sauce (recipe below).
6. Mix bread crumbs with melted butter and sprinkle over cheese sauce.
7. Bake at 375° F for 20 minutes. Do not over bake.

Cheese Sauce

3 tbsp	margarine or butter	45 ml
3 tbsp	all purpose white flour	45 ml
¼ tsp	salt	1 ml
¼ tsp	pepper	1 ml
2 cups	milk	500 ml
½ cup	cheddar cheese, grated	125 ml

1. To make roux, melt butter, whisk in flour, salt and pepper. Gradually, whisk in milk and cook in microwave, stirring frequently, until sauce is desired consistency.
2. Add grated cheese, stir until melted

Baked Cod Tongues
A heritage recipe as told to us by Rosalie Cabot.

24 cod tongues,
2 tbsp. salt
1 c. milk
1 c. biscuit or bread crumbs

Wipe cod tongues with damp cloth. Soak in milk in which salt is dissolved for about 10 minutes. Drain and roll in crumbs. Place on a greased sheet or dish and bake in 450° F oven for about 10 minutes. Serve with lemon slices.

Fried Cod Tongues
A heritage recipe as told to us by Ruby Cabot

Carefully wash fresh cod tongues and dry in paper towel. Allow 7 or 8 per person. Put 1 ½ cups flour, 1 tsp. salt. ½ tsp. pepper all together in a plastic bag. Put tongues in bag and shake them until evenly floured. Cut up ½ lb. Salt pork and fry until golden brown. Remove pork cubes and fry tongues in cooking oil until golden brown on both sides.

Fish Hash
A heritage recipe as told to us by Myrtle Jones.

This is an old fashion recipe that my mom, Martha Letto, used to do.

You take one medium cod, four or five potatoes, one onion, and about ¼ pound of salt pork.

You soak your salt cod overnight, until you think it's soaked enough and you boil it with the potatoes. Then you fry out your pork scrunchins' and you adds one finely chopped onion, you remove the fish and potatoes and you mashed your potatoes and you de-bone and skin your fish and you mix it all together. You add the scrunchins and onions and then you add a pinch of pepper and you mix it all together. And it's really good.

Working at the Fish
From a story told to us by Agnes Pike.

As soon as, we were old enough to be able to handle the fish or wash a dish or make a batch of bread, we was taught how to do that, or take a set of knitting needles in your hand, you know. That was the way of life, it was a part of our survival, I guess. And as a young girl, very young, I mean you were called out of bed early in the mornings when the men come in with a trap load of fish and get up and go down to the stage. And mom, her main job in the fishery was to salt her fish. She was a salter, but grandmother was a splitter - left handed splitter, and she taught me to split at a very young age. My first job was how to head the fish, I'm not very tall now, but at that time she stood me on one of those three quarter tubs about twelve or fifteen inches high and stood up to the table and taught you how to head a fish.

And you know it was nothing but work, I was probably eight or ten years old then. You went from that to helping to dry the fish and bring it in and one thing another. And then, when the fall of the year came, in the month of September, you went to school. You were up early in the mornings, help to spread the fish, 'til twenty minutes before school, you go up and wash your hands and perhaps get a slice of molasses bread and off to school. In the evenings, right out of school, get a lunch and right down at the fish again, 'til five o'clock or six o'clock.

Shrimp Curry Stir Fry

2 tbsp	oil	30 ml
2 cloves	garlic, finely minced	2
2 tbsp	curry powder	30 ml
2 tsp	turmeric	10 ml
1 stalk	celery, chopped	1
½	green pepper diced	1/2
½	red pepper, diced	1/2
2 cups	broccoli, chopped	500 ml
2 cups	cauliflower, chopped	500 ml
1 medium	Spanish onion, chopped	1
1 cup	snow peas	250 ml
1 lb	shrimp, peeled and deveined	454 g
Dash	Tabasco sauce	Dash
1 pkg	curry noodles, cooked & drained	1 pkg
	salt and pepper, to taste	

1. Heat oil in a wok. Add garlic and curry powder and turmeric. Cook for one minute.
2. Add vegetables and cook for about 5 minutes. Remove from pan, set aside and keep warm.
3. Add shrimp to wok and cook for approximately one minute.
4. Return cooked vegetables to wok with shrimp.
5. Add Tabasco sauce, cooked curry noodles and salt and pepper to taste. Serve immediately.

Fried Salmon

A heritage recipe as told to us by Marie Marshall

To prepare salmon for frying, split salmon down back, remove bone and stomach. Clean and wash well. Lay flat on a board and cover with coarse salt. Let stand for 1 hour then wash off salt and place on board and put outdoors in sun for about 1 hour to stiffen. It is now ready to cut into pieces for frying.

Salmon may also be fried as soon as it is cleaned and washed. Cut into pieces and dry in paper towels, roll in flour and place in lightly greased frying pan, add salt and pepper and fry until golden brown.

Boiled Salmon

A heritage recipe as told to us by Kathleen O'Brien

1 salmon, cut as desired
1 tsp. salt,
½ cup salt pork scraps

Boil salmon in salted water with salt pork until cooked through, approximately 20 minutes. Salmon may also be boiled with potatoes. If so, leave out pork and add salt to taste.

Cod Baked In Foil with Leeks and Carrot

Preheat oven to 450° F.

¼ cup	unsalted butter, softened	60 ml
1 ¼ tsp	finely grated lemon zest	7 ml
2	medium garlic cloves minced	2
½ tsp	minced thyme	2 ml
1 tsp	salt	5 ml
1/4 tsp	black pepper	1 ml
1 tsp	parsley	5 ml
2	medium carrots cut into matchsticks	2
2	medium leeks white and green parts cut into matchsticks	2
¼ cup	dry white wine	60 ml
4	skinless cod fillets each 1" to 1 ¼" thick	4
8	12" sheets foil	8

1. Combine butter, lemon zest, garlic, thyme, salt and pepper in small bowl. Set aside
2. Combine parsley remaining zest and remaining garlic in another small bowl. Set aside.
3. Place carrots, leeks in medium bowl. Season with salt and pepper and toss together. Set aside.
4. Arrange foil sheets on counter. Divide carrot and leek mixture among foil sheets, mounding in the center of each. Pour 1 tbsp of wine over each.
5. Pat fish dry with paper towels, season with salt and pepper, and place one fillet on top of each vegetable mound.
6. Spread quarter of butter mixture on top of each fillet.
7. Place second square of foil on top of fish. Crimp edges together in ½ inch fold. Then fold over three more times to create a pocket about seven inches square.
8. Bake 15 minutes in 450° F oven.

Crispy Oven Fried Fish

Preheat oven to 425° F

½ cup	all purpose flour	125 ml
	salt and pepper to taste	
	2 eggs	2
2 tsp	horseradish	10 ml
3 tbsp	mayonnaise	45 ml
¼ tsp	cayenne pepper	1 ml
1 cup	fine bread crumbs, with parsley or summer savoury	250 ml
1¼ lb	cod fillets washed, dried and cut in four pieces	550 g

1. Put ¼ cup flour, salt and pepper in a shallow dish or pie plate.
2. In another shallow dish or pie plate whisk eggs, horseradish, mayonnaise, and cayenne pepper. Whisk in 5 tbsp flour until mixture is smooth.
3. Put seasoned bread crumbs in third shallow dish or pie plate.
4. Dry fish with paper towel and season with salt and pepper. Working with one fillet at a time, dredge in flour and gently shake off excess. Coat with egg mixture. Coat all sides with breadcrumb mixture.
5. Spray wire rack with non-stick cooking spray. Transfer breaded fish to wire rack.
6. Place rack on cookie sheet.
7. Bake for 18 to 25 minutes.

Fish & Brewis & Scrunchions
A heritage recipe as told to us by Marie Marshall.

This is made from dried salt codfish. Remove bones and skin from the dried salt fish; cut fish into pieces. Cover fish with cold water and soak overnight. Split cakes of hard bread, soak overnight in cold water. In the morning, change water on fish, bring to a boil for 20 minutes or until fish is tender.

After fish begins to boil, put hard bread on stove in same water in which it has been soaked, add salt and bring to a boil over medium heat. Remove from heat and drain immediately. Keep hot.

For scrunchions; cut a piece of fat pork in tiny cubes and fry until they are golden brown, pour over fish and brewis like gravy.

Fisherman's Brewis
A heritage recipe as told to us by Ruby Cabot.

2 cups fat pork
5 cakes of hard bread (soaked in cold water until soft)
1 package fillets or fresh codfish

Fry fat pork until a little brown; add fish, cook until you can remove bones; add hard bread, bring to a boil, mash right way and serve. Can be cooked within 20 minutes.

Fish and Brewis with Homemade Bread
A heritage recipe as told to us by Myrtle Jones

That's one medium cod, three or four slices of homemade bread and about a ¼ pound of salt pork. You skin, and boil your cod. You cut up your cod into three or four pieces and you boil it and you add some salt to the water and you boil it. And while the fish is cooking, you fry out some pork scrunchins'.

So when the fish is cooked, you remove it from the pot, you pick out the bones and remove the skin. You add the fish to the pork with a small amount of water that the fish was boiled in - just a little bit, not a lot. Then you cut your three or four slices of homemade bread into cubes and you put it on top of the fish and you toss it lightly with the fish and the pork and the bread. And that's really good

Ice Fishing Trip
From a story told to us by Victor Stone.

We was troutin', just about all day, we were gettin' a scatter one and by and by, George said, he said "You got to go over there, in that little gulley there and bore a hole". "Nah," I said, "There's nar one over there, we didn't get none all the marning".   So he went over and he bore a hole, and when he bore a hole down, he hauled up the auger and he hauled up a trout on 'em and then they started to come up through the hole. "Well" I said, "George b'y what's I gonna do?" I said, "They're coming up through the hole".
And when I thought I got enough up, I put me foot over the hole and stopped them from coming up. Yeah.

Fried Capelin
A heritage recipe as told to us by Rosalie Cabot.

The capelin should be fresh. Wash them well in salted water. Pinch head off and pull out as much of the entrails as possible. Again wash in salted water. Dry on a clean cloth. Dip in flour and fry in hot fat. Season and serve with bread or mashed potatoes.

Smothered Cod Fish
As told to us by Phyllis Roberts.

First you melt two tablespoons of butter in your pot, then you cut up your onion and your pork and fry it out, nice and brown.   Then you put your fish in the pot and just leave it there for a few minutes, until it gets the pork and onions, sort of into the fish. And then you put one cup of water, in the pot. And, put your potatoes in, you don't cut up your potatoes, just put them in whole or if they're big potatoes, you can cut them half.

And then you put your salt and pepper over your fish and potatoes and then you let them all cook until the potatoes and the fish is done. And when the fish and that is done, you put some bread on top of your fish and potatoes. This takes up all the juice that's in the pot which goes through the potatoes and the fish, and you makes your bread right nice

Well, I learned this 'Smothered Fish' from mom, when we were growin' up eh. When dad and them use to come in from out in boat, dad and the boys, well we'd all go down on the wharf and we'd either put the fish into the splittin' table - little box on the splittin' table. Put it into the splittin' table in box and ....clevin' the fish and gut it. Probably go up in the stage and help him put it on the pile or something for to salt it. Then mom use to come down head the fish - the women use to go in the stage. And when they get all the fish done, well they'd be all up the house gettin' a 'mug up'.

A cup of tea and a few raisin buns. That's the 'mug up', what they use to call it. If it wouldn't be dinner time, they use to go up and get a 'mug up' they use to say. A cup of tea and some raisin buns. And then we'd bring up our fish ready to cook for our meal. And a lot of time, we use to have 'Smothered Fish'. It's nice and good.

Land & Sea

Fish Casserole

A heritage recipe as told to us by Marie Marshall.

2 cups cooked cod
1 ½ cups white sauce
2 tbsp. butter

4 hard cooked eggs
4 med. Sized cooked potatoes
½ cup day-old bread crumbs

Bone and flake fish and place half of it in bottom of a buttered casserole dish. Slice eggs and lay over fish. Cover with ½ of the white sauce. Cover with ½ of the potatoes, sliced. Repeat these layers again. Melt butter, add crumbs. Sprinkle over top of casserole. Bake in moderately hot oven, 400° F, about 20 minutes. Serves 6-8.

Fisherman's Fresh Fish Stew

A heritage recipe as told to us by Angela Fowler.

Ingredients: 4 slices of fat back, 5 pounds of fresh cod fish, 1 medium onion, potatoes, pepper to taste, water .

Place fat back in a pan. Fry out well. Clean your fish, wash and remove skin. Cut into 2 inch squares. Add fish to fat and then add sliced onions or chives, slice potatoes an inch thick and cover the fish with the potato slices, add seasoning. Add ¾ cups of boiling water and more if you need it. Cook slowly until the potatoes and the fish are tender, usually about ½ hour. Makes six servings.

Winifred's Fresh Fish Pie
A heritage recipe as told to us by Audrey Flynn

Ingredients:
4 to 5 pound of fresh fish (cleaned and cooked)
5 medium potatoes
1 medium onion chopped
1 small piece of salt pork (small pieces)
Pepper to taste

Fry pork and onions together. Put aside. Peel and cook potatoes. Drain and mash. Pick bones out of fish and add to potatoes with onion and pork. Add pepper.

Pie Crust:
2 ½ cups of flour
2 ½ teaspoons of baking powder
½ cup of butter
½ cup of shortening
½ cup of water

Make pastry. Fill with fish hash. Bake at 350 degrees until brown.

Fish Soufflé
As told to us by Angela Fowler.

3 ½ tbsp. butter, 2 cups milk, 3 ½ tbsp. flour, 1/3 cup bread crumbs, 1/8 tsp. Paprika, 2 cups cooked fish, 2/3 tsp. salt, 2 eggs.

Melt butter, add flour and when smooth, stir in milk. Cook until thickened. Add seasoning & crumbs. Cool. Add flaked fish to sauce & mix well. Stir in egg yolks, and stiffly beaten whites. Put in greased baking dish & bake in a moderately hot oven until firm.

Land & Sea

Turr* Stew With Paste
A heritage recipe as told to us by Phyllis Roberts

Ingredients:
Place pork in pot and fry until brown. Cut turr into pieces and place in pot. Cut up an onion and add to turr, cook until the turr is partly cooked. Add turnip and carrots. Add potatoes. Add water, just enough to keep from burning and make gravy.

Paste:
Flour with a bit of lard or shortening, add baking powder and mix together with a little water. Roll it out with a roller or roll with hand. Put on top of stew and place in oven and bake.

**Turr is a seabird, the common murre.*

Fish Pie
A heritage recipe as told to us by Angela Fowler.

Line a greased baking dish with mashed potato. Fill the dish with minced cooked codfish (salt or fresh). Cover generously with drawn butter and onions. Add another layer of mashed potatoes. Bake for 30 minutes in a slow oven.

Drawn Butter
A heritage recipe as told to us by Kathleen O'Brien

¼ c butter, 2 small onions, chopped, salt & pepper to taste,
2 ½ tbsp. flour, 1 ½ cup hot water

Melt butter in a small saucepan; add onions and cook for a few minutes over low heat. Then add the flour and mix well. Add hot water and cook until thickened, stirring constantly. Remove from heat and serve over salt fish and potatoes.

Portuguese Creamed Salt Cod

1 ½ lbs	dried salt cod, cut in 4 pieces	681 g
1	large onion, peeled and thinly sliced	1
5 tbsp	olive oil	75 ml
1 ½ lbs	potatoes, peeled and diced	681 g
¼ c	water	60 ml
1 ¾ cup	milk	435 ml
3 tbsp	unsalted butter	45 ml
3 tbsp	all purpose flour	45 ml
½ tsp	pepper	2 ml
1 ½ cups	18% coffee cream	375 ml

To prepare fish:
1. Soak salt cod in cold water overnight.
2. Drain, rinse well. Remove bones and skin. Discard.
3. With your fingers, pull the cod into small shreds, set aside.

1. In a large heavy skillet set over very low heat, sauté the onion in 3 tbsp (45ml) of the olive oil for about 15 minutes, until very soft and golden, stirring occasionally.
2. Add cod and ½ cup (125ml) milk.
3. Cover and cook over lowest heat, stirring occasionally for 30 minutes. Remove from heat and keep warm.
4. Meanwhile, stir the potatoes in the remaining oil in a second large heavy skillet over moderately low heat for about 2 minutes, or until they begin to colour.
5. Add the water, turn the heat to lowest point, cover and cook 15 minutes. Remove from heat, set aside.

While cod cooks, prepare white sauce:
1. In a small heavy saucepan over moderate heat, melt unsalted butter
2. Whisk in flour and the remaining milk. Stir constantly until thickened and smooth, about 3 minutes. Add pepper, set aside and keep warm.

When cod has only 10 minutes more to cook, preheat oven to 450° F.
1. When cod is cooked, mix in potatoes, white sauce and cream. Transfer to a buttered shallow 9" x 13" casserole or *au gratin* pan.
2. Bake uncovered for 15 minutes.
3. Lower the temperature to 350° F and bake uncovered 25 minutes or until bubbly and tipped with brown.
4. Serve at once with a green salad.

Baked Cod Fillets with Stuffing

Preheat oven to 350° F.

2 lb	boneless cod fillets	1 kg
2 cups	fine bread crumbs	500 ml
1 tsp	salt	5 ml
1 tsp	pepper	5 ml
¼ cup	onions, diced	60 ml
1 tsp	summer savoury	5 ml
2 tbsp	melted butter	30 ml
½ cup	water	125 ml
¼ cup	salt pork, finely diced _or_	60 ml
¼ cup	vegetable oil	60 ml

1. Wash fish and pat dry on paper towel.
2. To make stuffing mixture, combine all other ingredients together except salt pork or oil.
3. Put salt pork or oil in the bottom of a casserole dish.
4. Add a layer of fish, alternating with stuffing mixture and ending with small amount of stuffing mixture, sprinkled over top.
5. Cover and bake 45 minutes 350° F.
6. If desired, serve with cheese sauce. (Below)

Cheese Sauce

3 tbsp	margarine or butter	45 ml
3 tbsp	all purpose white flour	45 ml
¼ tsp	salt	1 ml
¼ tsp	pepper	1 ml
2 cups	milk	500 ml
½ cup	cheddar cheese, grated	125 ml

1. To make roux, melt butter, whisk in flour, salt and pepper. Gradually, whisk in milk and cook in microwave, stirring frequently, until sauce is desired consistency.
2. Add grated cheese, stir until melted.
3. Serve with baked cod fillets with stuffing.

Mushroom Stuffing for Trout or Salmon

¼ cup	butter	60 ml
1/3 cup	chopped celery	80 ml
1/3 cup	minced onions	80 ml
1 cup	mushrooms, sliced	250 ml
1 tbsp	chopped parsley	15 ml
¾ cup	crushed crackers or fine bread crumbs	285 ml
¼ tsp	summer savoury	1 ml
¼ tsp	dried dill	1 ml

1. Melt butter and sauté onions and celery 3 to 4 minutes.
2. Add mushrooms and cook 2 minutes.
3. Remove from heat, stir in remaining ingredients.

Baked Salmon

A heritage recipe as told to us by Rosalie Cabot.

1 Whole salmon, 1 onion, chopped, 2 tbsp. melted butter,
2 cups bread crumbs, 1 tsp. poultry seasoning, 1 tsp. salt

Clean and dry fish; leave head and tail on but remove eyes. Make stuffing and sprinkle cavity of fish with salt. Stuff and skewer fish and sew up. Dot fish with butter or strips of fat pork. Wrap in foil and bake 1 hour at 350° F. Open foil for last minute of cooking.

Seafood Casserole

Stock:

4 cups	water	1 litre
1	medium onion, chopped	1
1 stalk	celery, chopped	1
1 small	carrot, diced	1
1 tsp	salt	5 ml
½ tsp	pepper	2 ml
1	bay leaf	1
¼ cup	all purpose flour	60 ml
¼ cup	butter	60 ml

To make stock:

1. In medium saucepan, combine all ingredients and boil for 5 to 10 minutes.
2. Strain through cheese cloth. Discard solids.
3. Return stock to saucepan, whisk in flour and butter. Heat, stirring constantly until thickened. Set aside

½ lb	sea scallops, cut in half	227 g
1 lb	cod fillets	454 g
1 can	clams	284 ml
1 cup	shrimp	250 ml
1	salmon fillet	170 g
½ cup	white wine	125 ml
2 cups	cooked noodles	500 ml
¼ cup	sundried tomato, chopped	60 ml
8 oz	fresh mushrooms, sliced	250 g
½ cup	cheese, grated	227 g
½ cup	fine bread crumbs	125 ml

1. Put all fish in medium skillet. Add wine and poach, until just cooked (approximately 8 minutes).
2. Break cod and salmon into bite size pieces. Add all the cooked fish and noodles to sauce.
3. Pour into greased casserole dish, top with bread crumbs and cheese.
4. Bake at 350° F until cheese is melted.

Boiled Porcupine

A heritage recipe, as told to us by Bill Goudie.

Ingredients:
½ porcupine
1 large onion
1 piece of salt beef or salt pork (5 inch square)
3 cups of water
1 teaspoon of pepper
3 or 4 medium potatoes

Cook porcupine, onion, beef or pork, pepper and water together. As the water boils off the porcupine, add up to 3 cups more. If more water is used it will take the taste of porcupine away. Cook for about 2 ½ hours. ½ hour before it is cooked, you add the potatoes and a dumpling.

Dumpling Recipe:
2 cups of flour
2 teaspoons of baking powder
teaspoon of salt
1 cup of cold water

Mix together and place dough over the porcupine and cook for about 12-15 minutes.

Flicko
A recipe cooked over the fire while in the country hunting, or cutting wood.
Told to us by Warren Fowler

Ingredients: Fat back pork, 3 partridges (or spruce partridges), 1 onion, 1 loaf of bread (crumbled)

Fry your fat back pork. Cut partridges into pieces and place into the pork. When the partridge is cooked, fry up onions with it. Put water over it. Then place pieces of bread into mixture and stir until it becomes "sappy". The number of partridges cooked usually reflects the number of people eating (4 people eating 4 partridges).

Lingonberry (Partridgeberry) Meat Balls

Preheat oven to 350° F

2	eggs	2
1 cup	cornflake crumbs	250 ml
1 1/3	cup ketchup	330 ml
2 tbsp	soy sauce	30 ml
1 tbsp	parsley flakes	15 ml
2 tbsp	onion flakes	30 ml
½ tsp	salt	2 ml
¼ tsp	pepper	1 ml
2 lb	lean ground beef	1 kg
1 Cup	Pure Labrador Lingonberry (Partridgeberry) Spread	250 ml
3 tbsp	brown sugar	45 ml
1 tbsp	fresh lemon juice	15 ml

1. In a large bowl combine eggs, cornflake crumbs, 1/3 cup of ketchup (reserve 1 cup), soy sauce, parsley flakes, onion flakes, salt, pepper and ground beef.
2. Shape into balls (approximately 72 balls).
3. Place in pan and bake for 20 to 25 minutes at 350° F. Drain on paper towel. Discard any remaining fat in the pan.
4. In saucepan combine Pure Labrador Lingonberry (Partridgeberry) Spread, reserved ketchup, brown sugar and lemon juice. Stir constantly until Pure Labrador Lingonberry (Partridgeberry) Spread is melted.
5. Add to meat balls and heat thoroughly.

The Flynn Family's Weekly Menu

Typical menu growing up would be fish. You had to do something with cod fish and then there was salmon, then there was herring, then you had your jigs dinner and your stews and your soups.

Sundays, it was wild meats, your caribou, your turrs, and ducks.

Monday, it would be leftovers. Supper time it would be some sort of fish, it could be stewed, it could be fried or it could be baked, stuffed baked cod.

Then Tuesdays, it would be stew or soup.

And on Wednesday, it'd be beans, or baked beans, or stewed beans.

Thursdays, it was jigs dinner. The big meal was at dinner time, well lunch time we call it now but then it was dinner time and supper we had, you'd still have something cooked. It could have been fish again.

And Fridays, it was a fish day.

Saturday at Mom's house it was baked beans for supper, and pea soup for dinner - a windy day. Mom always had pea soup and baked beans.

And Sunday then it was your cooked dinner with your turrs or your wild meat.

Ethel Flynn

Caribou Roulade in Juniper Sauce

½ lb	ground caribou	227 g
1 slice	smoked ham	1
4 to 5 slices	bacon	4 to 5
1	onion, finely chopped	1
1	egg	1
1 cup	fine bread crumbs	250 ml
1 tsp	parsley	5 ml
2 lb	sliced caribou meat, flattened with a cleaver	1 kg

1. Combine ground caribou, smoked ham, bacon, onion, egg, bread crumbs, and parsley.
2. Mix well. Put 2 Tbsp (30ml) on each flattened slice of caribou. Roll and secure with toothpick.
3. Dredge rolls in seasoned flour. Brown on all sides in hot oil.
4. Place browned rolls in baking pan. Set aside.

Sauce:

3 ½ cups	beef consommé	900 ml
1 cup	dry red wine,	250 ml
1 small can	tomato sauce	
1 clove	garlic mince,	1
1 tbsp	juniper berries	15 ml

1. Combine all sauce ingredients and pour over rolls.
2. Cover and bake at 350° F for 1 ½ hour or until tender.

Caribou Stew

2 tbsp	vegetable oil	30 ml
2 lbs	caribou cubed	1 kg
2 cups	carrot diced	500 ml
1 cup	celery chopped	250 ml
1	large onion, chopped	1
2 cups	turnip diced	500 ml
4 cups	potatoes diced	1 L
	Water	
	Salt and pepper to taste	

1. Heat oil in a deep pot and add caribou. Season with salt and pepper, sauté until browned. Add a little water and simmer until meat is tender.
2. Add vegetables and enough water to see in pot around vegetables.
3. Simmer for about 30 minutes or until vegetables are tender.

Beef a la Deutsch

1	onion finely chopped	1
1	garlic clove, finely chopped	1
	butter (or oil) for frying	
½ lb	fresh mushrooms washed and sliced	227 g
1	green pepper finely chopped	1
¼ cup	red wine	60 ml
1 can	consommé	284 ml
	salt and pepper to taste	
1	bay leaf	1

1. Sauté onions and garlic in small amount of butter; add mushrooms and green pepper. Cook for 5 minutes.
2. In small saucepan combine wine, consommé, salt, pepper and Bay Leaf, simmer for 5 minutes. Set aside and keep warm

3lb	beef tenderloin tips	1.5 kg
	salt and pepper to taste	
	olive oil or grapeseed oil	

1. Sauté tenderloin tips in hot oil until well browned.
2. Drain oil from pan, season beef with salt and pepper.
3. Cover with sauce and simmer to blend flavours

Please note: Although this recipe calls for tenderloin, it also can be used with a less expensive cut of meat and baked in the oven for approximately 2 ½ hours at 325° F.

Pork Chops with Lingonberry (Partridgeberry) Mustard Sauce

2 tbsp	olive oil	15 ml
4 - 6	boneless pork chops	4 - 6
1	medium onion, chopped or sliced	1
1 cup	Pure Labrador Lingonberry (Partridgeberry) Spread	250 ml
1/3 cup	Dijon mustard	80 ml
¼ tsp	each ground ginger, nutmeg, and black pepper	125 ml
½ tsp	salt	2.5 ml

1. Heat 1 tbsp (15 ml) oil in frying pan over medium heat. Brown pork chops on both sides, remove to baking dish.

2. Add remaining oil and sauté onion 3 minutes or until tender.

3. In small saucepan, stir together Pure Labrador Lingonberry Spread, mustard, ginger, nutmeg, pepper and salt. Bring to boil and pour over the pork chops.

4. Bake uncovered in a 350° F oven for 20 to 25 minutes depending on thickness of chops. Turn pork chops once during baking.

Chicken or Pork Chop Casserole

Preheat oven to 350° F.

6 pc	chicken or 6 pork chops	6
1	small onion, chopped	1
	salt and pepper to taste	
¾ cup	converted rice	185 ml
½ tsp	Italian seasoning	2 ml
½ tsp	dried basil	2 ml
1 tsp	dried oregano	5 ml
1	chicken bouillon cube	1
1 ¼	cup water	310 ml
1 can	golden mushroom soup	284 ml

1. Place chicken or pork chops in a greased casserole dish.
2. Add onions and salt and pepper.
3. Put uncooked rice over meat.
4. Sprinkle Italian seasonings over rice.
5. In a small bowl, dissolve chicken bouillon in water and combine with Golden Mushroom soup. Pour this mixture over chicken or pork chops and rice. Bake 1 to 1 ½ hours.

Cloudberry (Bakeapple) Glazed Chicken Breast

4	chicken breasts	4
1 tbsp	butter, melted	15 ml
2 tsp	lemon juice.	10 ml

1. Blend melted butter and lemon juice.
2. Dip each chicken breast in this mixture.
3. Season with Montreal Chicken Spice.
4. Cook over medium heat until barely pink.
5. Put in ovenproof glass dish.

Glaze:

¾ cup	Pure Labrador Cloudberry (Bakeapple) Syrup	185 ml
1 tbsp	custard powder	15 ml
¼ cup	cold water	60 ml

1. In small saucepan, heat syrup slowly.
2. Add custard powder to cold water.
3. Stir well and pour into hot syrup, stirring until thickened.
4. Pour over cooked chicken and bake at 350° F for 15 minutes.

Lingonberry (Partridgeberry) Glazed Chicken

Preheat oven to 350° F.

1	whole chicken, cut into pieces	1
3 tbsp	olive oil	45 ml
1 ½ Cup	Pure Labrador Lingonberry (Partridgeberry) Spread	375ml
¼ cup	soy sauce	60 ml
2 tbsp	lemon juice	30 ml
1 tsp	ground ginger	5 ml
1/3 cup	brown sugar	80 ml
1 tsp	dry mustard	5 ml
1	garlic clove minced.	1

1. Wash chicken, wipe with a damp cloth and pat dry.
2. In a large skillet, heat oil, and lightly brown chicken pieces on both sides for about 15 minutes.
3. Transfer chicken to a baking dish.
4. Combine remaining ingredients and pour over chicken.
5. Bake at 350° F for 45 minutes or until chicken is tender.

Pure Labrador Cloudberry (Bakeapple) Chicken Breast

2 lbs	boneless skinless chicken breasts	1 kg
2 tbsp	butter	30 ml
6 tbsp	finely chopped green onions	90 ml
6 tbsp	white wine vinegar	90 ml
9 tbsp	Pure Labrador Cloudberry (Bakeapple) Syrup	120 ml
6 tbsp	cream	90 ml
4 tsp	Pure Labrador Cloudberry (Bakeapple) Spread	20 ml

1. Flatten chicken breasts. Melt butter in frying pan over medium low heat. Sauté chicken breasts 3 minutes on each side. Remove from pan.

2. Add onion to frying pan, cover, and sauté over low heat for 1 2 minutes.

3. Add vinegar and Pure Labrador Cloudberry (Bakeapple) Syrup and simmer uncovered until reduced by half. Mixture should look thick and syrupy.

4. Whisk in cream.

5. Put breasts in sauce and simmer gently for 5 minutes. Do not overcook.

6. Place breast on plate, spoon 1 tsp (5 ml) Pure Labrador Cloudberry Spread on each breast. Then pour sauce over the breasts.   Yield: 4 servings

Ethel's White Bread

Yeast:

24 grams	yeast	24 g
2 cups	warm water	500 ml
1 tsp	sugar	5 ml
7 lb	all purpose white flour	3.18 kg
2 tbsp	salt	30 ml
1/3 cup	granulated white sugar	80 ml
½ cup	melted shortening	125 ml
7 to 8 cup	warm water	2 L

1. Dissolve sugar in warm water, sprinkle yeast over top. Let rest for ten minutes. Stir well.
2. While yeast is resting, mix together flour, salt, and sugar in a large bowl.
3. Mix melted shortening with warm water and add yeast.
4. Add liquid ingredients to dry ingredients and knead until dough is smooth and no longer sticky
5. Grease top with a little butter, cover and let rise in a warm space until double in size. Knead.
6. Cover again and let rise for 1 ½ to 2 hours. Knead again. Shape into loaves and place in greased pans, keep dough level at half full.
7. Cover and let rise until double in size, approximately 1 hour.
8. Bake 350° F for 40 minutes. Makes 7 or 8 loaves

Learning to Make Bread

"Well, I was nine year old when I started, cooking. My first batch of bread, I was nine. And from that, I think I was in the bread pan.

My mom was helping my dad put the fish away and it was really late one night when she got home from the stage head, so I decided I was going to make bread before she got home. And that's how I started. With the help of Grandfather Flynn, I think, he watched over me.

So that's how I started. "

Ethel Flynn

Blueberry or Partridgeberry Muffins

Prepare muffin pan either spray with cooking spray or line with muffin cups and spray with cooking spray. Preheat oven to 400° F.

2 ½ cup	all purpose flour	625 ml
¾ cup	granulated white sugar	180 ml
2 tsp	baking powder	10 ml
1 tsp	baking soda	5 ml
½ tsp	salt	2 ml
½ cup	butter or margarine	125 ml
1 cup	vanilla yogurt (at room temperature)	250 ml
2	eggs, slightly beaten	2
1 tsp	vanilla	5 ml
1 ½ cups	fresh or frozen blueberries or partridgeberries (if frozen, do not thaw)	375 ml

1. In large bowl mix flour, sugar, baking powder, soda and salt with pastry blender.
2. Cut in butter or margarine until mixture resembles fine crumbs.
3. Set aside.
4. In small bowl stir yogurt until creamy.
5. Blend in eggs and vanilla.
6. Pour wet ingredients into flour mixture and stir until just moistened.
7. Gently fold in blueberries.
8. Fill muffin cups two-thirds full and bake in preheated 400° F oven for 15 to 20 minutes.

Bread & Buns

Raisin Buns

As told to us by Rita Davis.

Ingredients:
4 cups of flour
¾ cup of sugar
6 teaspoons of baking powder
1 cup of butter
1 cup of coconut (fine coconut)
Very little salt 1/8 of a teaspoon full of salt

*Rub it all together like you would make
pie crust.*

Then take:
2 eggs and beat them into
¾ of cup of milk or water,
1 teaspoon of vanilla
1 cup of raisins or currents

Put it in a bowl and beat it with a wooden spoon into a soft dough. Put the dough on a rolling board and pat it out with your hands and take a small glass cut out the biscuits, nice and thick, maybe about an inch or inch and a half thick and put them on a cookie sheet and put them in the oven at 350 degrees. Bake them at ten or twelve minutes until they start to get brown

Be truthful we used more plain ones then we did raisins and currants when we were growing up. "Cause I guess, maybe it wasn't so easy to get, it was very special. At Christmas time, you would use all these fruit things but in between, you'd only just make the plain tea biscuit we would call it.

Well when I was growing up, probably about 8 or 9 years old, I always liked around the kitchen cooking and of course my mom and them spent a lot of time outdoors. They would go off berry picking or in helping my dad to make the hay and I would be the one to stay home and mind the kids, 'cause we were from a very large family, there was twelve in the family and I was second oldest. So she'd take what ones could help her in at the hay and that but I was the one that had to stay home with the kids and usually the older one, was the one, so that would be me.

And then one day, I'll never forget, we were going to have our dinner and of course we didn't have enough of bread for all of us for our dinner and some of the kids said, "Oh" and start to cry, "We don't have enough bread for dinner". I said, "Never mind, you give me a few minutes," and I said I wasn't long making up a pan of these plain tea biscuits and there's an old gentleman visiting our home at the time.

And of course, when my mom came back from being in the woods that day, he use to come over. "My dear, that little thing you got there", he said, "She wasn't long feeding them all dinnertime today," He said. "They didn't have enough bread," he said "And she made up a pan of buns, the fastest ones, ever I seen made."

Cheese Apple Scones

Preheat oven to 450° F. Grease baking sheet or line with parchment paper.

1 ¾ cup	all purpose flour	435 ml
2 tbsp	granulated white sugar	30 ml
1 ½ tsp	baking powder	7 ml
1/2 tsp	salt	2 ml
¼ tsp	baking soda	1 ml
1/3 cup	butter or margarine	80 ml
¾ cup	buttermilk	185 ml
1 cup	cheddar cheese, shredded	250 ml
1 cup	apple, peeled and diced	250 ml

1. Combine dry ingredients.
2. Cut in margarine until mixture resembles cornmeal.
3. Stir in buttermilk until moistened.
4. Fold in shredded cheese and apple.
5. Turn onto floured surface. Knead 10 times. Pat into 9" circle and cut into 8 wedges.
6. Separate and place on prepared baking sheet.
7. Bake at 450° F for 12 to 15 minutes.

Serve with Pure Labrador fruit spreads.

Bread & Buns

A Story about Making Bread
As told to us by Charlotte Flynn.

'Tis wonderful to know where your flour is, we are living in a world of wonderful age. Years ago when I was a young girl, flour was sometimes hard to find, I remember my mother, Effie Buckle and my Aunt Marion Trimm, they didn't have enough flour to make a batch of bread each, so they put two lots of flour together and made bread and when it was baked they halfed it. There was about five loaves each, today we haven't got to do that, we can go get our seven pound of flour and put it in the pan and we know where it all comes from. But them days it was hard, was hard them days.

Toutons
As told to us by Kathleen O'Brien

When white bread has risen and is ready to go in pans, break off small pieces about the size of an egg and flatten to around ½' inch thick. Drop in frying pan where fat back pork has been cut up and fried out until pork is crisp or can be fried in melted butter whichever is preferred. Brown on both sides and serve with butter and molasses or jam.

Making Doughnuts
As told to us by Diana Davis

Dad use to always go out and get his seals and bring 'em home and use them for food or whatever and then they used the seal skin for whatever he wanted him for, and then in the meantime, he'd take the fat off the skin and he'd bring it home and mom would put it in the big pot and put it on the stove. Render it all out and get the grease so when she got the grease now, she says "I'm gonna make some doughnuts, now, so to give you a treat". So anyway, mom set to work and made her doughnuts, so when we come home from school sure enough here was the doughnuts on the plate which she had cooked in seal fat.

And by the way, doughnuts was made out of flour and molasses and baking soda. And they just took them and rolled them out on a floured cookie sheet and they punched a little hole into them.

Lassy Coady Dumplings
A heritage recipe as told to us by Sylvia Buckle.

Ingredients:
1 ½	cups of flour
1 ½	tablespoons of shortening
3	teaspoons of baking powder
2/3	cups of water or milk
½	teaspoon of salt

<u>Dumplings:</u>
Mix dry ingredients together, cut in shortening finely. Add water or milk. Mix lightly with a fork. Drop dough by the spoonful over hot stew or hot vegetables. Cover and simmer for fifteen minutes. Don't remove cover.

<u>Coady:</u>
½ - 2 cups of Molasses
Bring molasses to boil in a sauce pan. Serve over hot dumplings.

Bread & Buns

Salt Pork Buns

As told to us by Olive Marshall

This is how this recipe goes: It's 4 cups of flour, and 1/3 pound of salt pork cup in fine cubes. 4 ½ teaspoons of baking powder, 1 cup of lukewarm water or enough to make tea buns consistently.

So you sift the flour and baking powder in a mixing bowl. Cut pork in fine cubes, rinse in warm water and partially fry in a pan. Cool the pork a little and pour pork, and fat driven from it, in a hollow made in the flour. Add lukewarm water and mix with hands to risen tea bun mixture. Make into buns and bake about ½ hour or until golden brown.

Now this recipe dated back oh, about a hundred years ago and it was mostly used by like grandfathers and great grandfathers and uncles. When they use to go for long trips in the interior. Like for huntin' caribou, you know, or the trappers when they went huntin' , and on trapping trips. They'd be gone a long time, they'd probably be gone six months, or four or six months or so before they come back, right? And then, also they were eaten by the kids at home, like for a snack. Because there wasn't always, the fancy biscuits, we have today and cookies or whatever, right?

This was a very old recipe, this one. I have a memory of next door neighbor, they make up plain old fashioned pork buns and they'd be gone in caribou huntin' - gone a good month or month at the time. That was as I remember.

And that's the way it'd go and they had the dog team too.   The dogs had their meal and dry capelin and whatever they mix up their dog meal. So they'd take that with them, I suppose. So the dog could have their meal, because they use to be gone a long time. I remember next door neighbor and his brother and them, they'd be gone probably, a good six weeks, I remember that.

So imagine, way back before his time, his great grandfather, or his grandfather, or his father before him. He had a dog team, from about eight or nine dogs. They'd dress up, they had the meal for the dogs, and then they'd pack it on the komatik with the coachbox, right. And they use to take their stove with 'em. 'Cause I guess, I don't know what they had for shelter - tent or something made out of that cotton duck. I remember they had a half forty five gallon drum, made like a stove or old tin stuff or something - had a stove and a couple stove pipes on it and along with all their grub. Full load. Dogs had to be taken care of.

And I use to help make the harnesses for the dogs - made out of rope. We use to sew the flannelette around 'em. And make the tossels. Make different color tossels for each dog. Right? So they are all dressed up to take off on the trip. So I guess that's where the old fashioned buns make up enough for them to take, however long they were gone.

Pork Bangbellies
A heritage recipe as told to us by Sylvia Buckle.

Ingredients:
2 cups of molasses
1 teaspoon of baking soda
1 pound of salt pork
1 teaspoon of spice
1 teaspoon of nutmeg
4 cups of flour

Heat molasses on stove. Cut pork in small cubes and fry. Add to molasses while hot and dissolve baking soda in boiling water. Add spice to flour. Mix well together and bake. Grease pan and lay rind of pork on bottom of pan. Eat while warm.

Partridgeberry Muffins (With Variations)

Preheat oven to 350° F. Grease muffin cups, or line with paper liners and spray with cooking spray.

2 ¼ cups	all purpose flour	560 ml
2 1/2 tsp	baking powder	7 ml
¾ cup	granulated white sugar	180 ml
¼ tsp	salt	1 ml
1	egg	1
1 cup	orange juice	250 ml
1/3 cup	melted butter	80 ml
1 tsp	almond flavouring	5 ml
1 cup	partridgeberries, fresh or frozen	250 ml
	(If frozen, do not thaw)	

1. Mix dry ingredients in a large bowl.
2. Separately beat egg into orange juice, add flavouring.
3. Make well in dry ingredients, add egg/orange juice and flavouring.
4. Add melted butter and berries. Minimal mixing.
5. Bake at 350° F about 15 minutes. Test to see if baked, if not continue baking, checking at 5 minute intervals. Because they are quite moist when put in muffin pan, I find these take a little longer to bake.

Note: This recipe can also be the base for many other muffins: apple, banana or blueberry. To enhance the flavour of blueberry muffins, add 1 tbsp (15ml) pure lemon juice and 1 tbsp (15ml) pineapple juice.

Topping for apple muffins: ¼ cup (60ml) brown sugar; ¼ cup (60 ml) chopped nuts; ½ tsp (5ml) cinnamon. Sprinkle topping over muffins before baking.

Bread & Buns

Partridgeberry-Orange Quick Bread

Preheat oven to 350° F. Grease and prepare 9 ½" x 5"x 3" loaf pan

2 cups	sifted all-purpose flour	500 ml
¾ cup	granulated sugar	185 ml
1 ½ tsp	baking powder	7 ml
1 tsp	salt	5 ml
½ tsp	soda	2 ml
1 cup	partridgeberries, fresh or frozen (if frozen, do not thaw)	250 ml
½ cup	chopped walnuts	125 ml
1 tsp	freshly grated orange zest	5 ml
1	beaten egg	1
¾ cup	orange juice	185 ml
2 tbsp	salad oil	30 ml

1. Sift dry ingredients together
2. Stir in partridgeberries, nuts and zest.
3. Combine egg, orange juice and salad oil
4. Add to dry ingredients, stirring just until moistened.
5. Bake in greased 9 ½ x 5 x 3 inch loaf pan at 350° F for 50 minutes or until done.
6. Remove from pan to cool.

Coconut Tea Buns

Preheat oven to 400° F.

4 cups	all purpose flour	1 litre
¾ cup	granulated white sugar	185 ml
2 tbsp	baking powder	30 ml
1 cup	coconut	250 ml
½ tsp	salt	2 ml
1 cup	margarine	250 ml
2	eggs	2
1 cup	milk	250 ml

1. Blend dry ingredients well.
2. Cut in margarine until mixture resembles cornmeal.
3. Beat together eggs and milk. Add to flour mixture.
4. Turn onto floured surface and pat into rectangle ½ inch deep. Cut into rounds.
5. Bake at 400° F for 12 to 14 minutes. Do not over bake.
   Serve with Pure Labrador fruit spreads.

Partridgeberry Loaf

Preheat oven to 350° F

2 cups	all purpose flour	500 ml
1 tsp	baking powder	5 ml
1 tsp	baking soda	5 ml
1 tsp	cinnamon	5 ml
1 tsp	allspice	5 ml
½ cup	butter	125 ml
1 cup	granulated white sugar	250 ml
2	eggs	2
1 tsp	vanilla	5 ml
1 cup	milk	250 ml
1 cup	raisins	250 ml
1 cup	partridgeberries, fresh or frozen, (do not thaw)	250 ml
½ cup	chopped walnuts	125 ml

1. Sift together first 5 ingredients.
2. Cream butter and sugar. Beat until light and fluffy.
3. Add eggs, one at a time beating well after each addition.
4. Add vanilla.
5. Add dry ingredients to creamed mixture alternately with milk.
6. Fold in raisins, berries and nuts.
7. Pour into greased medium tube pan. Bake at 350° F for 50 to 70 minutes.

White Bread without Yeast
A heritage recipe as told to us by Olive Marshall.

Ingredients:
Steep out hops and use 2 cups of the liquid.*
1 cup of warm water
1 teaspoon full of sugar
2 cups of scalded milk
5 teaspoons of salt
¼ cup of sugar
10 to 12 cups of sifted all purpose flour
¼ cup melted butter or shortening

Mix ingredients together into a dough and let rise. Then divide dough into buns and place in greased bread pans and let rise. Then bake.

** The hops in this recipe is identified as green spruce cones.*
Olive says this recipe was used long before yeast was available in Labrador.

Memories of my Mom

"My memories of my mom, things that she taught me to do, was bake and to be kind to other people. When I was nine, that's when she started to teach me how to mix bread. She would always put the ingredients together and then she'd let me mix it and, by the age of eleven, I was totally mixing bread on my own. And I'm still mixing bread.

My mom was very kind and you know if she knew somebody was in need of something and she had it. She would take the last, for example a can of milk or when we didn't have can milk, we had cows, she'd give the last bottle of milk or the last can of milk away. If she knew somebody was in need."

Nancy Flynn

Pure Labrador Baked Alaska Lingonberry (Partridgeberry) or Cloudberry (Bakeapple) Pie

1	9" baked pie shell	1
4 oz	cream cheese	113 g
¼ cup	granulated white sugar	60 ml
1 litre	vanilla ice cream, softened	1
1 ½ cups	Pure Labrador Cloudberry (Bakeapple) Spread _or_ Lingonberry (Partridgeberry) Spread	375 ml

1. Cream together cream cheese and sugar until smooth and fluffy. Fold in vanilla ice cream
2. Spread in baked pie shell, wrap and freeze. (This can be stored in the freezer up to 2 months.)

Just before serving preheat oven to 450° F.

Meringue

3	egg whites	3
¼ tsp	cream of tartar	1 ml
1/3 cup	granulated white sugar	80 ml

1. Beat egg whites until stiff and dry.
2. Combine cream of tartar with white sugar and slowly add to beaten egg whites.
3. Completely cover frozen pie with meringue being careful to have it touch all the way around edge of pastry.
4. Bake in preheated oven until lightly browned.

Puddings & Pies

Lingonberry or Cloudberry Cream Puffs

Grease baking sheet and Preheat oven to 400° F.

½ cup	butter or margarine	125 ml
1 cup	boiling water	250 ml
1 cup	all purpose flour	250 ml
¼ tsp	salt	1 ml
4	eggs	4
	unsweetened whipped cream	
1	jar Pure Labrador Cloudberry (Bakeapple) _or_	325 ml
	Lingonberry (Partridgeberry) Spread	

1. In medium saucepan melt butter in boiling water.
2. Combine flour and salt and add all at once, stirring vigorously.
3. Cook and stir until mixture forms a ball that doesn't separate. Remove from heat: cool slightly.
4. Add eggs, one at a time, beating after each addition, about 1 to 2 minutes or until smooth.
5. Drop batter by heaping tablespoon 3 inches apart onto greased baking sheet.
6. Bake at 400° F about 30 minutes or until golden brown and puffy.
7. Remove from the oven and split, removing any soft dough.
8. Cool on wire rack.
9. Fill with unsweetened whipped cream and Pure Labrador Cloudberry (Bakeapple) or Lingonberry (Partridgeberry) Spread.

Fluffy Cloudberry (Bakeapple) Rice Pudding

¾ cup	uncooked long grain rice	185 ml
¼ cup	granulated white sugar	60 ml
4 cup	milk	1 litre
¼ cup	dry milk powder	60 ml
1 ½ tsp	vanilla	7 ml
¼ tsp	almond flavouring	1 ml
½ cup	whipping cream	125 ml
1 jar	Pure Labrador Cloudberry (Bakeapple) Spread	250 ml
	whipped cream to garnish	

1. In heavy 2 quart saucepan, combine uncooked rice and sugar. Stir in milk.
2. Bring mixture to a boil. Reduce heat. Cover and cook 20 to 25 minutes or until rice is tender, stirring occasionally.
3. Stir in dry milk, vanilla, and almond extract.
4. Cool to room temperature.
5. Whip cream to soft peaks.
6. Fold whipped cream into rice mixture cover and chill thoroughly.

To Serve:
1. Spoon rice pudding into dessert dishes and put Pure Labrador Cloudberry (Bakeapple) Spread over each serving.
2. Garnish with small dollop of whipped cream
Makes 6 to 8 servings.

Apple Pudding

A heritage recipe as told to us by Gertie Fowler.

2 tbsp butter
¼ cup sugar
1 cup flour
1 tsp baking powder
1 pinch salt
1 cup chopped apple
6 tbsp of milk

Mix everything together. Put the batter in a large bowl because it will rise in the bowl.
Then make the filling and pour over the batter.

 Filling;
1 cup brown sugar
1 teaspoon butter
1 ½ cups boiling water
1 teaspoon vanilla

Bake at 375° F for 35 minutes.
This is a pudding that I made for my family many evenings for supper.
I serve it with ice cream. You can always find the ingredients in your kitchen.

Lingonberry (Partridgeberry) Stuffed Baked Apples

4	apples	4
½ cup	Pure Labrador Lingonberry (Partridgeberry) Spread	125 ml
3 tbsp	walnuts, toasted and finely chopped (optional)	45 ml
Pinch	cinnamon or nutmeg	Pinch

Preheat oven to 425° F.

1. Core apples leaving some apple on the bottom (A melon baller works well for this).
2. Mix together Pure Labrador Lingonberry Spread, walnuts, and spice. Fill apples.
3. Place apples in baking dish and bake 15 - 20 minutes or until tender.
4. Serve warm with whipped cream, custard or ice cream.

Hersilia's Berry Tarts

Preheat oven to 350° F. Prepare tart pans by spraying with cooking spray or lining with small muffin cups that have been sprayed with cooking spray.

1 cup	butter	250 ml
2 cups	all purpose flour	500 ml
3 tbsp	brown sugar	45 ml
	Pure Labrador Cloudberry (Bakeapple), Lingonberry (Partridgeberry) or Blueberry Spread	
	whipped cream	

1. Blend butter, flour and brown sugar well.
2. Form into small balls and put in prepared tart pans.
3. With fingers, shape each ball into a tart.
4. Bake until lightly browned, approximately 10 minutes.
5. Cool slightly and remove from pans
6. Fill with Pure Labrador Spread of choice
7. Garnish with dollop of whipped cream

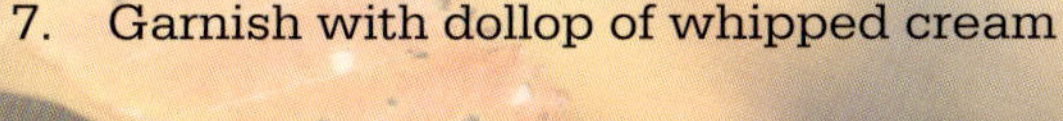

Lingonberry (Partridgeberry) Pecan Pie

1	9-inch baked pie crust	1
½ cup	Pure Labrador Lingonberry (Partridgeberry) Spread	125 ml
2 cups	pecans, coarsely chopped	500 ml
3	large eggs	3
½ cup	granulated white sugar	125 ml
1 cup	light corn syrup	250 ml
5 tbsp	butter, melted	75 ml
1 tbsp	dark rum _or_	15 ml
1 tsp	vanilla	5 ml

1. Spread the Lingonberry (Partridgeberry) spread evenly over the baked pie crust.
2. Place the pecans on a cookie sheet and toast in a 375° F oven for 6 to 10 minutes or until fragrant. Set aside to cool.
3. In a large bowl whisk together the eggs, sugar, corn syrup, and butter. Stir in the pecans.
4. Pour over the Lingonberry (Partridgeberry) Spread in the prepared pie shell and bake until the edges are firm and the center seems set but quivery, 35 to 40 minutes.
5. Remove from oven and let cool at least 1 ½ hours. Serve warm or at room temperature with whipped cream or ice cream. Yield: 1 9-inch pie

Partridgeberry Pie
A heritage recipe as told to us by Ruby Cabot

Recipe: One pastry recipe for a 9 inch pie shell.
Roll out dough and place on a shallow plate such as a dinner plate. Spread around 1 cup or a little more sweetened partridgeberry jam on dough and cover with pastry strips. Bake at 425° F for 10 minutes. Reduce heat to 350° F. and bake for 20-25 minutes.

Pastry
A heritage recipe as told to us by Kathleen O'Brien

2 c. Flour, 1 tbsp. sugar, pinch of salt, 1 c. butter, ½ tsp. baking powder, ¼ cup water. Mix with a fork and roll.

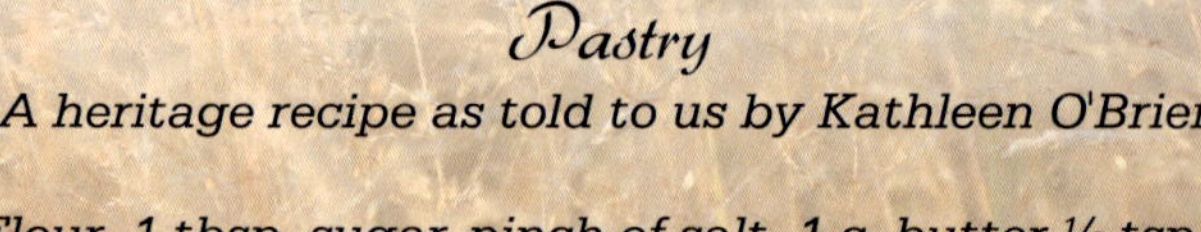

Puddings & Pies

Molasses Pudding

A heritage recipe as told to us by Gertie Fowler

½ cup butter
2 eggs
1 cup sugar
1 cup berries
2 cup molasses
2 cups hot water
6 cups flour
2 tsp cloves
3 tsp baking soda
4 tsp cinnamon

Cream butter, sugar, eggs and molasses.
Add flour, cloves, and cinnamon.
Dissolve soda in the hot water and add to the mixture, then add the berries.
Pour into a greased pudding bowl and steam for 2 ½ hours.
Serve with sauce or gravy.

I make this pudding every Christmas and steam it in 1lb butter tubs, (the recipe makes 8 small puddings), then give them to my friends to add to their Christmas dinner. Most of them serve the pudding with gravy over it.

Molasses Pies
A heritage recipe as told to us by Grace Normore.

1 cup molasses
½ cup water
1 tsp cinnamon
½ tsp spice
½ tsp cloves
2 cups bread crumbs

Bring to a boil, molasses, water, cinnamon, spice, cloves, thicken with bread crumbs.

Crust: (rub together)
2 ½ cups flour
2 tsp baking powder
½ cup shortening
½ cup butter
½ cup water
1 egg
2 tsp vanilla
¼ cup sugar
Pinch of salt.

Add water egg and vinegar to the dry ingredients;
roll out the dough to make the pie.
Cut strips of pastry to put on top of
the molasses filling.
Bake at 370° F for 15 to 20 minutes.

Baked Partridgeberry Pudding & Caramel Sauce

Preheat oven to 325° F. Grease 9" x 13" pan.

2/3 cup	butter	160 ml
1 ½ cup	granulated white sugar	375 ml
2	eggs	2
1 tsp	vanilla	5 ml
2 cup	all purpose flour	500 ml
2 tsp	baking powder	10 ml
½ tsp	salt	2 ml
1 cup	milk	250 ml
1 cup	partridgeberries, fresh or frozen (if frozen, do not thaw)	250 ml

1. Cream butter and sugar together until light and fluffy.
2. Add eggs, one at a time and beat thoroughly after each addition. Add vanilla.
3. Combine flour, baking powder, and salt, blending well.
4. Add dry ingredients alternately with milk to creamed mixture.
5. Fold in partridgeberries.
6. Pour into prepared 9" x 13" pan. Bake at 325° F for 45 to 50 min. Serve with Caramel Sauce (below)

Caramel Sauce

1 cup	brown sugar	250 ml
1 ½ cup	boiling water	375 ml
Pinch	salt	Pinch
1 tbsp	custard powder	15 ml
2 tbsp	cold water	30 ml
2 tbsp	butter	30 ml
1 tsp	vanilla	5 m

1. To make syrup: bring sugar, water and salt to a boil.
2. Mix custard powder with cold water. Add to syrup. Bring to a boil.
3. Add butter and vanilla. Keep warm

Rhubarb and Strawberry Pudding

Preheat oven to 375° F

½ cup	granulated white sugar	125 ml
3 cup	rhubarb	750 ml
1 cup	strawberries	250 ml
¾ cup	granulated white sugar	185 ml
2 tbsp	butter	30 ml
1	egg	1
½ tsp	vanilla	2 ml
1 cup	all purpose flour	250 ml
2 tsp	baking powder	10 ml
½ cup	milk.	125 ml

Sauce:

1 cup	water	250 ml
1 tbsp	butter	15 ml
2/3 cup	granulated white sugar	160 ml

1. Combine ½ cup sugar, rhubarb and strawberries and put in a greased 8"x8" dish.
2. Cream butter and sugar. Add egg and vanilla and blend well.
3. Combine flour and baking powder, whisk well to blend.
4. Add alternately to creamed ingredients with milk.
5. Spread over rhubarb/strawberry mixture.
6. **To prepare sauce**: In small saucepan, bring to a boil water, butter and sugar. Pour over pudding.
7. Bake at 375° F for 45 minutes.

Cow's Milk Bread Pudding
As told to us by Kathleen Cabot.

First I'm going to tell about the cow's milk bread pudding. Mom used eggs in the pudding if and when the hens would lay eggs because we always had eggs too.
And we had cows for many years. I remember some people in L'Anse au Loup, who come to moms on Sundays for a bottle of cow's milk and cream and maybe her older friends, or ladies would come for a lunch and she would serve them also partridgeberry jam, with homemade bread and cow's cream, which was delicious.

Back in those days if you had dried up bread well you would not throw it away. It was always used for something. So this is a recipe for the bread pudding:

8 cups cow's milk
1 cup white sugar
2 tablespoons vanilla
6 or 8 slices of butter bread so this would mostly be dried up bread and then we'd cut the bread in pieces and they would butter the top of the bread.

Then they put the milk in a deep pan or dish, stir in the sugar and vanilla and they would cut the bread into small pieces and add liquid mixture. And they would bake it at 350 degrees, uncovered for 45 minutes.

And when it was baked it would be nice and brown and crispy on the top and we would love it because mom would serve it to us then with the cow's cream on the pudding which was very delicious. It wouldn't be served as a dessert, maybe sometimes it would be served as a meal.

Mostly I think it would be around dinner time they would do that and as I remember, especially Sunday evenings, we would have it for supper. I guess it was some kind of a treat that was served like, as we would call now, dessert, but we would have it as a meal for Sunday evening for supper especially.

Puddings & Pies

Millicent's Pastry for Pies

4 cups	all purpose flour	1 litre
4 tsp	baking powder	20 ml
8 oz	margarine	227 g
8 oz	shortening	227 g
1	egg	1
1 tsp	vinegar	5 ml
	water	

1. Sift together flour and baking powder in large bowl.
2. Cut margarine and shortening into dry ingredients, until the mixture is the size of peas.
3. In measuring cup, beat egg well. Add vinegar and enough water to measure 1 cup (250ml).
4. Combine with flour mixture. Minimal mixing.
5. If pastry is too soft, add a little more flour to make desired consistency.
6. Roll out on lightly floured pastry board and line greased pie plate.
   Yield: 4 two crust pies

Hard Bread (Hard Jack) Pudding
A heritage recipe as told to us by Olive Marshall.

Ingredients:
4 cakes of hard bread
1 teaspoon of pepper
1 onion
¼ pound of salt pork

Soak hard bread overnight. Strain and mash it. Chop the onion fine and add to the mashed bread. Add pepper, put in a pudding bag and tie it tightly. Boil for two hours with jigs dinner. Serve with molasses or corn syrup, if used for a dessert.

Partridgeberry or Bakeapple Shortcakes

Preheat oven to 375° F

2 cups	all purpose flour	500 ml
4 tsp	baking powder	20 ml
1 tbsp	white granulated sugar	15 ml
½ tsp	salt	2 ml
½ cup	shortening	125 ml
1	egg	1
1/3 cup	milk	80 ml
1/3 cup	sour cream	80 ml
	Pure Labrador Lingonberry (Partridgeberry) *or*	
	Pure Labrador Cloudberry (Bakeapple) Spread	
	Whipped cream	

1. In a large mixing bowl, combine flour, baking powder, sugar and salt. Cut in shortening until well mixed.
2. In small mixing bowl, combine egg, milk, and sour cream.
3. Add to flour mixture until blended. Minimal mixing. Turn out onto a floured surface, pat into a rectangle ½" thick and cut into rounds. Bake at 375° F for 10 to 15 minutes or until golden brown. Do not over bake.
4. To serve top warm or cooled biscuit with Pure Labrador Lingonberry (Partridgeberry) *or* Pure Labrador Cloudberry (Bakeapple) Spread. Garnish with dollop of whipped cream.

Puddings & Pies

Steamed Partridgeberry Pudding

Prepare container: Grease container (choose from the small heatproof mixing bowl of the mix-master, coffee cans, or a 6-cup/1.5 litre pudding mould). The lid must fit tightly. If using the mixing bowl, grease waxed paper and put over top, then add a layer of tin foil and anchor it all with a wide elastic band. As pudding will rise, fill container only ½ full.

½ cup	margarine	125 ml
1 cup	granulated white sugar	250 ml
1	egg	1
2 cups	all purpose flour	500 ml
1 tsp	baking soda	5 ml
1 tsp	baking powder	5 ml
¾ cup	milk	185 ml
2 cups	partridgeberries, fresh or frozen. (if frozen, do not thaw)	500 ml

1. Cream butter and sugar. Add egg. Beat well.
2. In separate bowl, mix flour, baking soda, baking powder and add alternately to creamed mixture with milk.
3. Gently fold in berries.
4. Turn the mixture into the prepared container. Secure the lid. Place on a wire rack in the bottom of a large stock pot with a tight fitting lid. Add enough boiling water to come halfway up the side of the container. Cover the pot with a lid and bring the water to a low simmer. Steam for 2 to 2 ½ hours. Check water often and <u>do not allow to go dry.</u>
5. Remove the pudding from the pot and cool to room temperature before unmoulding

Note: The pudding can be made ahead to this point. It will keep in plastic wrap for 2 days in the refrigerator or 2 weeks in the freezer.

To serve, place the pudding back in the mould and steam in the stock pot for 30 minutes or until heated through. Serve with heated Lemon Sauce (facing page).

Lemon Sauce

¼ cup	butter or margarine	60 ml
1	egg (well beaten)	1
1 cup	icing sugar	250 ml
¼ cup	lemon juice (or to taste)	60 ml

1. Melt butter or margarine in top of double boiler.
2. When melted, pour in slowly 1 well beaten egg, stirring constantly to prevent sticking.
3. Add sugar. Stir with whisk to make sure no lumps.
4. Add lemon juice and continue to stir until well blended.
5. Keep warm in top of double boiler. If sauce thickens before you're ready to use it, slowly add a little water to reach desired consistency

Seaview Restaurant Pineapple Bread Pudding

Preheat oven to 350° F.

4	eggs	4
4 cups	milk	1 litre
¾ cup	granulated white sugar	375 ml
1 cup	crushed pineapple and juice	250 ml
1 tsp	vanilla	5 ml
3 tbsp	melted butter	45 ml
10 slices	white bread, crusts removed and cut into cubes	10

1. Beat eggs. Add milk, sugar, pineapple, vanilla, and melted butter.
2. Put bread cubes in 9" x 9" glass baking dish. Cover with egg mixture.
3. Place dish in a large pan with 1 ½ to 2" water.
4. Bake at 350° F for one hour

Blueberry Pudding
A heritage recipe as told to us by Blanche Bridle.

Ingredients:
1 ¾ cups of flour
3 ½ teaspoons of baking powder
¼ cup of butter
1 cup of sugar
1 egg
7/8 cup of water
4 tablespoons of milk
1 teaspoon of vanilla
2 cups of blueberries

Cream butter, sugar. Beat eggs until thick and light. Add milk, add dry ingredients and water. Beat until smooth. Add vanilla and berries. Bake at 350° F for 30 minutes.

Sauce for Pudding

1 cup of brown sugar
3 tablespoons of flour
¼ teaspoon of salt

Gradually stir in two cups of boiling water. Boil until smoothly thickened. Remove and stir in 2 tablespoons of butter and ½ teaspoons of vanilla. Stir constantly, until it gets thick.

Partridgeberry Crumb Square

Bottom:

¾ cup	butter	185 ml
1 ½ cup	all purpose flour	375 ml
1/3 cup	icing sugar	80 ml

1. Cream butter and icing sugar until light and fluffy. Beat in flour.
2. Press into 13" x 9" pan. Bake 10 to 12 minutes at 350° F.
3. Remove from oven and turn oven to 325° F.

Second Layer:

1 pkg	cream cheese	250 g
1 can	condensed milk	300 ml
¼ cup	lemon juice	60 ml
2 ½ cups	Pure Labrador Lingonberry (Partridgeberry) Spread	625 ml
2 tbsp	cornstarch	30 ml
1 tbsp	brown sugar	15 ml

1. In large bowl beat cream cheese until fluffy.
2. Add condensed milk and blend until smooth. Stir in lemon juice.
3. Pour over crust.
4. In same bowl combine corn starch and Labrador Lingonberry (Partridgeberry) Spread and brown sugar.
5. Mix well and spoon over cheese mixture.

Topping:

¾ cup	butter	185 ml
¾ cup	all purpose flour	185 ml
1 cup	brown sugar	250 ml
1 cup	pecans	250 ml
1 cup	rolled oats	250 ml

1. In medium bowl mix brown sugar and flour, cut in cold butter until crumbly.
2. Add nuts and rolled oats.
3. Sprinkle over partridgeberry mixture.
4. Bake at 325° F for 30 to 35 minutes.
5. Cool and cut into squares

Aunt Martha's Blackberry (Crowberry) Pie
As told to us by Myrtle Jones.

Now I got one here, "Aunt Martha's Blackberry Pie". This is my mother's. I made a little story out of this and it goes back to when I was a little girl, when she use to say, "Now it's time to go berry picking".

You go out on the barrens and pick a ½ gallon of blackberries. You get the children to go and help. Now you're back and being it's a hot day, you might have let the fire die down, so someone has to go to the woodpile and get a pan of chips to get the fire going. Now you get out the old iron pot and get the berries cooking.

Add water and sugar to taste and boil until the berries are cooked.

Then you measure about four or five cups of flour because this is going to be a supper meal, four or five teaspoons of baking powder and a pinch of salt.

You melt a ½ cup of lard, now you mix your flour, your baking powder and salt and make a hole in the middle. You add the melted lard and enough water to make a dough that's easy to roll.

You takes half of the dough, roll the size of the diameter of the pot that you're cooking it in and you put that piece of dough into the pot and you push it down into the jam. You take the other half and you rolls that the same size. Then you'll make a hole in the center of that with your finger so that the berries will come up through and go right over the top of it.

You put that directly on top of the first dough, so you cook that for about fifteen to twenty minutes or until it's done.

Blueberry Sour Cream Cake

Preheat oven to 350° F.

Base:

1 ½ cups	all purpose flour	375 ml
½ cup	granulated white sugar	125 ml
½ cup	butter	125 ml
1	egg	1
1 tsp	vanilla	5 ml
3 cups	blueberries	750 ml

1. Blend flour, sugar and butter.
2. Add egg and vanilla until mixed well.
3. Spread batter in 10 inch spring foam pan.
4. Pour 3 cups blueberries over base.

Topping

2 cups	sour cream	500 ml
1	egg	1
½ cup	granulated white sugar	125 ml
1 tsp	vanilla	5 ml

1. Blend all ingredients.
2. Spread over blueberries.
3. Bake at 350° F for one hour.

Cloudberry (Bakeapple) Ginger Tart

Crust

2 cups	ginger snaps, finely ground	500 ml
½ cup	butter, melted	125 ml

Filling

8 oz	cream cheese	227 g
3 tbsp	sugar	45 ml
3 tbsp	milk	45 ml
1 tbsp	crystallized ginger, finely chopped	15 ml
Pinch	salt	Pinch

Topping

1 cup	Pure Labrador Cloudberry (Bakeapple) Spread	250 ml
2 tbsp	cloudberry liqueur (optional)	30 ml

1. **Crust:** Combine the crumbs and butter. Press into a 9-inch spring form pan. Bake 8 to 10 minutes in a 350° F oven. Cool completely.

2. **Filling**: Beat all ingredients together until light and fluffy. Spread into cooled crust and refrigerate until firm.

3. **Topping:** Combine the ingredients and spread evenly over the cream cheese filling. Refrigerate. Yield: one 9-inch tart.

Berryocky, a Christmas Drink
A heritage recipe as told to us by Rita Davis

Ingredients: 1 Quart Bakeapples or Partridgeberries, 4 cups Water

In a saucepan boil berries until they are cooked. Add 2 cups of cold water and 2 cups of sugar or to taste. Let cool and store in a cold place.

I remember when we were young this is what we gave to our friends and jannies in Christmas. We would serve it with Buns or Molasses cake. The jannies would say they wanted clinging, we knew that this was a way of asking for a drink of berryocky and a lunch.

Partridgeberry Tea

6 cups	water	1.5 L
2 cups	Pure Labrador Lingonberry (Partridgeberry) Spread	500 ml
1	cinnamon Stick	1
4	cloves	4
6 cups	apple juice	1.5 L
	fresh lemon wedges	

1. In a large stainless steel pot, bring water to boil and add Pure Labrador Lingonberry (Partridgeberry) Spread, cinnamon stick and cloves.
2. Reduce heat and simmer for 20 minutes.
3. Add apple juice, stir well and serve hot over lemon wedge.

Partridgeberry Punch

4 cups	partridgeberries	1 litres
6 cups	water	1.5 litres
2 cups	granulated white sugar	500 ml
3 tbsp	pure lemon juice	45 ml
1 cup	orange juice	250 ml
1 litre	ginger ale or 7-Up	1 litre

1. Cook Partridgeberries in 4 cups (1.5 litres) water until soft. Crush and strain through cheese cloth.
2. Dissolve sugar in remaining 2 cups (500 ml) water and boil for 5 minutes.
3. Add to partridgeberry juice and chill.
4. Add fruit juices.
5. Just before serving add ginger ale or 7-Up.

Partridgeberry Milkshake

Mix in blender:

1 cup	skim milk	250 ml
1 large scoop	vanilla ice cream	1
½ cup	partridgeberries	125 ml

Spruce Beer
As told to us by Elzear O'Brien.

Well the way we use to make spruce beer, and I heard of a lot of other people made it handy about the same thing.

We'd get a gallon of spruce water, and then you'd get a pack of yeast, if you was just only making a gallon. Well, you get a pound of white sugar, and a cup of raisins and some people most times would cut up a potato and a half cup of raisins would go into that. Everything to put a taste on it.

And then you'd cut the boughs, and then some other people would probably put rice into it. Everything would get into it 'fer to make a good taste on it.

And then you'd cut the boughs of the spruce wood and you'd cut the boughs into small pieces. You didn't have to cut it, but you could limb it off, rhine it off with your hand or whatever 'fer to get the small pieces. And then you'd put that into a large boiler and you'd cover the boughs with the water. If you had a gallon or if you were making two gallons, whatever it was. And then you'd let that boil for a hour and when it was boiling for an hour, you figured it was boiled good enough and then you'd take it off the stove and you'd let it cool down a bit.

After it was cool enough to handle, well you'd strain it then through a cheese cloth to get all the twigs and that out of the beer, whatever it was into it. And then you'd put the liquid into a jar, a gallon jar, if you had it, and you'd let it brew then for eight to ten days.

Some people now use to put spruce buds into it too. They said it use to make a better taste on your spruce beer. So when everything was worked, after eight or ten days and everything was settled to the bottom of the jar, you knew it was finished, so then you'd take your beer and you'd bottle it. And most times if you get beer bottles, you'd put it in beer bottles to make it look a bit better anyway for drinking.   A lot of people use to use those quart bottles, we'd call them Mason jar bottles. Anything at all to hold your beer in. Especially when you know a time coming up or something, you had a couple of bottles of beer to take with you. But that's the recipe they use to use for the spruce beer anyway.

People use to drink it for medicine - drink a tumbler full or something. But most people use to make it fer to get a bit of alcohol out of it I guess. That was the big thing to it.

Well that's the story I knows about it anyway.

Christmas Partridgeberry Chutney

7 cups	partridgeberries	1.75 litres
1 cup	raisins	250 ml
3 cups	water	750 ml
2 cups	granulated white sugar	500 ml
1 tbsp	cinnamon	15 ml
1 ½ tsp	ground ginger	7 ml
¼ tsp	cloves	1 ml
3	apples (pared, cored and chopped)	3
1 ½ cups	celery, chopped	375 ml
2 med	onions, chopped	2
½ tsp	nutmeg	2 ml

1. Put berries, raisins and water in large saucepan and cook for 20 to 25 minutes over medium heat.
2. Mix together sugar, cinnamon, ground ginger and cloves; stir into berries and raisins.
3. Add apples, celery and onion.
4. Continue to cook for approximately 15 minutes on medium heat. Watch carefully to prevent burning and lower heat to simmer for another 10 minutes. Break the berries as Chutney cooks.
5. Remove from heat and add nutmeg.
6. Put into prepared preserving jars and store Chutney for at least a week in order to allow flavours to develop.

(Freeze in small containers if desired)

Partridgeberry Chutney

3 cups	partridgeberries	750 ml
1 cup	dried apricots, chopped	250 ml
½ cup	dates, chopped	125 ml
½ cup	onion chopped	125 ml
½ cup	cider vinegar	125 ml
½ cup	light corn syrup	125 ml
¾ cup	brown sugar	310 ml
1 tbsp	grated orange peel	15 ml
¾ cup	orange juice	185 ml
2 tsp	dry mustard	10 ml
½ tsp	salt	2 ml
¼ tsp	ground ginger	1 ml

1. In a large heavy saucepan, combine all ingredients. Bring to a boil.
2. Reduce heat and simmer, uncovered for 15 to 20 minutes or until thickened.
3. Chill.
4. Serve as an accompaniment to turkey or pork. Makes about 3 ½ cups.

Blueberry Marinade

6 tbsp	Pure Labrador Blueberry Syrup	90 ml
2 tsp	fresh gingerroot, peeled and finely grated	10 ml
4 tsp	fresh lemon juice	20 ml
1 tbsp	soy sauce	15 ml
1	clove garlic, minced	1
	salt and pepper, to taste	

1. Blend together all ingredients.
2. Use as marinade on meat, poultry, fish, tofu or vegetables

Rhubarb Relish

4 cups	rhubarb	1 litre
4 cups	onions	1 litre
2 cups	vinegar	500 ml
1 ½ lb	granulated white sugar	680 g
1 tsp	salt	5 ml
1 tsp	allspice	5 ml
1 tsp	cinnamon	5 ml
1 tsp	cloves	5 ml
1 tsp	pepper	5 ml

1. Combine rhubarb, onions and vinegar. Let rest overnight.
2. In large saucepan, cook until tender.
3. Add sugar and salt and continue to cook for a further 10 to 15 minutes.
4. Add spices and pepper and simmer together for 10 minutes. Stir frequently.
5. Put in sterilized jars.

Shrimp Pate

1 can	tomato soup	284 ml
8 oz	cream cheese	227 g
1 cup	mayonnaise or whipped dressing	250 ml
1 ½ pack	gelatin dissolved in 3 tbsp (45 ml) water	
1 cup	onion	250 ml
1 cup	celery	250 ml
1 cup	salad shrimp	250 ml

1. Heat soup and add cream cheese, stirring until melted.
2. Remove from heat. Whisk or blend in blender until smooth consistency.
3. Add Miracle Whip and gelatin. Whisk until blended.
4. Cool to room temperature. Add shrimp, celery and onion.
5. Serve with crackers.

Shrimp Dip

8 oz pkg	cream cheese	227 g
½ cup	mayonnaise or whipped dressing	125 ml
1 ½ cup	salad shrimp	375 ml
½ tsp	onion powder or chopped green onion	2 ml
1 tsp	Worcestershire sauce	5 ml
	seafood sauce	
	crackers	

1. Beat cream cheese, add mayonnaise or whipped dressing and continue to beat until smooth. Stir in remaining ingredients. Chill.
2. Just before serving put seafood sauce over top
3. Great served with crackers.

Baked Brie in Phyllo with Partridgeberry Preserves and Pecans

Preheat oven to 375° F. To prepare cookie sheet, spray with cooking spray.

4	sheets frozen phyllo dough	4
1	Brie	227 g
½ cup	Pure Labrador Lingonberry (Partridgeberry) Spread	125 ml
½ cup	pecans, chopped.	125 ml
	Selection of fresh fruit	
	Small baguette slices; crackers	

1. Brush each sheet of phyllo with melted butter and carefully stack one on top of each other. Trim stack into a 13" or 14" square.
2. Trim off any wax or peel from outside of Brie, leaving the edible rind intact.
3. Position Brie in the center of the phyllo, and brush top of Brie with melted butter.
4. Top with Pure Labrador Lingonberry (Partridgeberry) Spread
5. Add chopped pecans
6. Fold one 4-ply stack phyllo over Brie, partridgeberry spread, and pecans. Repeat procedure with the remaining sides until you have a phyllo package. Brush entire surface of package with melted butter and push corner edges inward to mold package into a round.
7. Position phyllo, seam side down, in centre of prepared cookie sheet. Bake at 375° F for 30 minutes.
8. Allow to stand a few minutes, transfer to serving plate. Set aside for 5 minutes. Garnish edge of platter with slices of fresh fruit and sliced baguettes.

Partridgeberry French Toast Casserole

2 tbsp	softened butter, to grease baking dish	30 ml
8	large eggs	8
2 tbsp	maple syrup	30 ml
3 ½ cups	milk	875 ml
1 tsp	pure vanilla	5 ml
½ tsp	salt	2 ml
½ tsp	cinnamon	2 ml
¼ tsp	nutmeg	1 ml
1 loaf	day old bread, torn into pieces	1
1 cup	fresh (or frozen) partridgeberries	250 ml
	if frozen, do not defrost	
	Pure Labrador Lingonberry (Partridgeberry) Syrup	

Grease a 9 x 13 inch baking dish

1. In a large bowl, whisk eggs, maple syrup, milk, vanilla, salt, cinnamon and nutmeg until thoroughly combined.
2. Gently stir in the bread pieces and the partridgeberries.
3. Let the mixture stand for 15 minutes. Give it a little stir, then spoon into the prepared baking dish.
4. Cover with plastic wrap and refrigerate overnight.
5. Next day, preheat the oven to 350° F.
6. Remove the wrap and bake for 35 to 40 minutes or until the casserole is puffed, lightly browned and when poked with a finger in the middle, the casserole is firm to the touch. Serves 8.

Serve with Pure Labrador Lingonberry (Partridgeberry) Syrup.

Cloudberry (Bakeapple) Crepes

1 cup	all purpose flour	250 ml
Pinch	salt	Pinch
1	egg, beaten	1
1 ¼ cup	milk	310 ml
2 tbsp	butter melted	30 ml
	Pure Labrador Cloudberry (Bakeapple) Spread	
	Whipped cream	

1. Sift the flour and salt into a large bowl and make a well into the center. Combine beaten egg and milk. Add gradually to dry ingredients and whisk until the batter is smooth and free of lumps. Cover. Set aside for 30 minutes.
2. Transfer the batter to a jug for easy pouring.
3. Heat a small crepe or non stick frying pan and brush lightly with melted butter.
4. Pour a little batter into the pan, swirling to thinly cover the pan. If the batter is too thick add 2 to 3 teaspoons (10 to 15ml) of milk. Cook for about 20 seconds.
5. Transfer to a plate and cover with wax paper. Continue to cook and stack the crepes between wax paper to prevent them from sticking together. Keep warm.
6. To serve, fill each crepe with Pure Labrador Cloudberry (Bakeapple) preserves, to taste, and garnish with whipped cream.

Blueberry Pancakes

¼ cup	vegetable oil	60 ml
2	eggs	2
¾ cup	plain yogurt	185 ml
½ cup	milk	125 ml
½ cup	apple juice	125 ml
¼ cup	liquid honey	60 ml
1 ½ cup	all purpose flour	375 ml
1 ½ tsp	baking soda	7 ml
½ tsp	salt	2 ml
¼ tsp	cinnamon	1 ml
1 cup	blueberries, fresh or frozen, (if frozen, do not thaw)	250 ml

1. In large bowl, whisk together oil, eggs, yogurt, milk, apple juice, and honey.
2. In separate bowl, mix together flour, baking soda, salt and cinnamon. Add to egg mixture and stir just until dry ingredients are moistened.
3. Heat greased griddle over medium heat. Using three tablespoons of batter for each pancake, drop batter onto griddle.
4. Sprinkle blueberries over pancakes. Cook for about three minutes or until bottom is golden and bubbles break on top.
5. Turn and cook until bottom is golden brown.
   Serve with Pure Labrador Blueberry Syrup.

Chocolate Buttermilk Waffles with Strawberries

1 cup	all purpose flour	250 ml
2/3 cup	granulated white sugar	160 ml
½ cup	cocoa powder	125 ml
¾ tsp	cinnamon	3 ml
½ tsp	baking powder	2 ml
½ tsp	baking soda	2 ml
1 cup	buttermilk	250 ml
2	eggs, separated	2
¼ cup	melted butter	60 ml
½ tsp	vanilla	2 ml

1. In a large bowl, mix together flour, sugar, cocoa, cinnamon, baking powder, and baking soda.
2. Make well in center and pour in buttermilk, egg yolks, melted butter and vanilla. Whisk into flour mixture.
3. In separate bowl beat egg whites until soft peaks form, fold one quarter of this into batter. Fold in remaining whites.
4. Heat waffle machine and cook according to manufacturer's directions, using 1/3 cup (80 ml) batter for each waffle.

Topping:

3 cups	strawberries (fresh or defrosted)	750 ml
1 ½ tbsp	white granulated sugar	22 ml
	whipping cream or plain yogurt to taste	

1. Stir together strawberries and sugar.
2. Top each waffle as desired and garnish with a dollop of whipped cream or plain yogurt

Strawberry and Poppy Seed Salad

Dressing

½ cup	sour cream	125 ml
1 tbsp	granulated white sugar	15 ml
1 tsp	freshly grated orange peel	5 ml
2 to 3 tbsp	milk	30 to 45 ml
1 tbsp	orange juice	15 ml

1. Whisk together sour cream, sugar, orange peel, milk and orange juice.
2. Set aside.

To caramelize pecans:

½ cup	chopped pecans	125 ml
2 tbsp	granulated white sugar	30 ml

1. In medium skillet, combine pecans and sugar.
2. Cook over medium heat, stirring constantly until sugar is melted and pecans are cooked and lightly browned.
3. Spread over wax paper, let cool.

Salad

3 cups	romaine lettuce	750 ml
3 cups	spinach	750 ml
2 cups	strawberries	500 ml

1. Just before serving, toss together caramelized pecans, romaine, spinach and strawberries in a large salad bowl.
2. Serve with dressing.

Apple, Walnut and Blue Cheese Salad with Lingonberry (Partridgeberry) Vinaigrette

4 servings	mixed baby salad greens	4
1	apple	1
¼ cup	walnuts, toasted and coarsely chopped	60 ml
¼ cup	crumbled blue cheese	60 ml

1. Spread a bed of salad greens on 4 plates.
2. Core and quarter the apples. Thinly slice each quarter into 6 to 8 slices and place on the greens in an attractive fan.
3. Sprinkle 1 tbsp (15 ml) each walnuts and blue cheese over the apple and greens.
4. Drizzle the Lingonberry Vinaigrette over the salads. Serves 4.

Lingonberry (Partridgeberry) Vinaigrette

3 tbsp	Pure Labrador Lingonberry (Partridgeberry) Syrup	45 ml
1 tbsp	red wine vinegar	15 ml
3 tbsp	olive oil	45 ml
	Salt and pepper to taste	

1. Combine all ingredients and whisk until well blended.

Ham and Potato Salad

4 cups	cooked potatoes, diced	1 L
2 tbsp	onion, finely chopped	30 ml
½ tsp	salt	2 ml
1/8 tsp	pepper	5 ml
½ cup	celery, chopped	125 ml
¼ cup	French dressing	60 ml
2	hard boiled eggs, chopped	2
¼ cup	green pickle relish	60 ml
1 tbsp	parsley	15 ml
1 ½ cups	cooked ham, chopped	375 ml
¾ cup	mayonnaise	185 ml

1. Combine potato, onion, salt and pepper and celery in large bowl.
2. Toss together gently and add French dressing. Cover and chill for about 2 hours.
3. Before serving add relish, eggs, parsley, and ham. Toss lightly.
4. Fold in mayonnaise and serve.

Alma's Bean Pie

Cora Barney shares her mother's recipe with us.
Her mother would serve this pie to guests at Christmas time.

Ingredients:
3 cups white beans
3 cups salt beef (cut into cubes)
2 large onions
3 cups potatoes (cut into cubes)
pepper to taste

In a boiler or large saucepan put the white beans, cover them with cold water, let boil for 1/2 an hour. Turn down the heat and let simmer for 3 hours.

Put salt beef in a saucepan cover with water and let boil. Strain it and cover with water again. Let cook for about 3 hours, then add to the beans and also add the onions. Let cook for 1/2 an hour, then add the potatoes. The beans has to be a little dry.

Ingredients for pastry
2 1/2 cups flour
1/2 tsp salt
2 tsp baking powder
1/2 cup shortening
1/2 cup butter
1/2 cup cold water
1 egg
2 tsp vinegar
1/4 cup sugar

Bake pie at 400° F for 15 to 20 minutes or until golden brown.

Lingonberry (Partridgeberry) Glazed Pork Loin

4 lb	pork loin	2 kg
½ cup	Pure Labrador Lingonberry (Partridgeberry) Glaze	125 ml
	salt and pepper	

Lingonberry (Partridgeberry) Glaze

6 tbsp	Pure Labrador Lingonberry (Partridgeberry) Syrup	90 ml
1 ½ tsp	salt	7 ml
1 ½ tsp	black pepper	7 ml
1 clove	garlic, minced finely	1
2 tsp	gingerroot, peeled and finely grated	10 ml
1\4 tsp	tomato puree	20 ml
2 tsp	Dijon mustard	10 ml
4 tsp	fresh lemon juice	20 ml

Blend together all ingredients. Yield: ½ cup (125 ml)

1. Marinate the pork loin with half the glaze overnight.
2. Preheat the oven to 375° F.
3. Season the pork loin with salt and pepper and sear the roast in a hot frying pan.
4. Place the pork loin in a roasting pan and brush with the remaining glaze. Place in preheated oven and bake until internal temperature reaches 145o F, approximately 45 to 50 minutes, basting often with the pan juices.
5. Remove from oven. Keep it warm and let it rest 20 minutes before carving.
6. Serve with Pure Labrador Lingonberry (Partridgeberry) Spread. Makes 6 to 8 Servings.

Boneless Leg of Lamb with Raspberry Sauce

Preheat oven to 350° F. Spray roasting pan with cooking spray

	boneless leg of lamb roast, well trimmed	
½ tsp	salt	2 ml
¼ tsp	pepper	1 ml
¼ cup	all purpose flour	60 ml
10 oz	frozen raspberries	280 g
1 tbsp	red currant jelly	15 ml
1 tsp	fresh lemon juice	5 ml
2 tsp	freshly grated lemon peel	10 ml
1 tbsp	Kirsch	15 ml
1 tbsp	cornstarch	15 ml
1 tbsp	water	15 ml

1. Combine salt, pepper and flour in plastic bag. Put roast in bag and dust with flour mixture.
2. Place in prepared roasting pan and bake at 350° F for 40 minutes
3. **To prepare sauce:** In small saucepan over medium heat, stir together berries, currant jelly, lemon juice, peel and Kirsch. Heat but do not boil.
4. Mix cornstarch and water and gradually pour into heated berry mixture. Stir constantly.
5. Pour ½ of the sauce over lamb and return to oven. Bake 30 minutes and baste occasionally.
6. Turn oven to 400° F and bake an additional 10 minutes.
7. Serve with remaining sauce.
   Yield: 4 servings.

Cloudberry (Bakeapple) Pecan Cake

1 cup	pecans	250 ml
3 cups	sifted all-purpose flour	750 ml
1 tsp	salt	5 ml
1 tsp	baking soda	5 ml
1 tsp	baking powder	5 ml
½ cup	Pure Labrador Cloudberry (Bakeapple) Syrup	125 ml
½ cup	milk	125 ml
1 cup	butter or margarine, room temp	250 ml
1 cup	granulated white sugar	250 ml
½ tbsp	orange zest	7.5 ml
1 tsp	vanilla	5 ml
4	large eggs	4
½ cup	Pure Labrador Cloudberry (Bakeapple) Spread	125 ml

Glaze:

½ cup	Pure Labrador Cloudberry Syrup	125 ml
2 tbsp	Cloudberry Liqueur or orange juice	30 ml

Preheat oven to 350° F.
Grease and flour 10 to 12 cup bundt pan.

1. Toast pecans in 350° F oven 10 minutes. Cool and chop finely. Set aside.
2. Mix together flour, salt, baking soda, and baking powder. Set aside.
3. Combine Pure Labrador Cloudberry Syrup and milk. Set aside.
4. Put butter, sugar, orange zest and vanilla in mixing bowl. Beat until light and creamy.
5. Add eggs, one at a time, beating well after each addition.
6. Beat in Pure Labrador Cloudberry Spread.
7. Mix in flour mixture alternately with milk mixture, ending with flour mixture.
8. Stir in pecans.
9. Pour into bundt pan and bake 55 to 60 minutes or until cake tester comes out clean when inserted into the middle of the cake. Let cool in pan 10 to 15 minutes. Meanwhile make the glaze by combining the syrup and liqueur.
10. Turn the cake out onto a rack. With a skewer or fork, poke holes all over the cake. Brush glaze over cake until it is all absorbed.

Partridgeberry Walnut Orange Muffins

Preheat oven to 400° F. Prepare muffin pans by spraying with cooking spray or insert large muffin cups sprayed with cooking spray.

2	oranges	2
1 cup	walnuts, chopped	250 ml
1 cup	partridgeberries (fresh or frozen)	250 ml
	(if frozen, do not thaw)	
1/3 cup	butter melted	80 ml
1	egg	1
2 cups	all purpose flour	500 ml
1 tbsp	baking powder	15 ml
½ tsp	salt	2 ml
2/3 cup	granulated white sugar	160 ml
	plus 1 tsp for topping	5 ml

1. Grate zest from oranges and measure 4 teaspoons (20 ml) into medium size bowl. Add walnuts and partridgeberries and stir to combine.
2. Squeeze juice from oranges and add water to measure 2/3 cup (160ml). Whisk together juice, cooled melted butter and egg until blended.
3. In a large bowl mix flour, baking powder, salt and 2/3 (160 ml) cup sugar.
4. Add liquid ingredients and stir until blended. Do not over mix. Fold in partridgeberries, orange zest and nuts
5. Spoon batter into 12 muffin cups. Sprinkle tops with remaining, 1 tsp (5ml) of sugar.
6. Bake in 400° F oven for 15 minutes. Test to see if baked and if not, continue checking at 5 minute intervals until done.

Thimble Cookies

Preheat oven to 350° F.

1	egg	1
½ cup	butter	125 ml
¼ cup	granulated white sugar	60 ml
2 tsp	lemon juice	10 ml
1 cup	all purpose flour	250 ml
1 cup	chopped walnuts	250 ml

Pure Labrador Blueberry, Lingonberry (Partridgeberry),

Cloudberry (Bakeapple), or Blueberry Spread

1. Separate egg.
2. Cream together butter and sugar. Beat egg yolk well and add lemon juice. Add alternately to creamed mixture with flour. Combine until well blended.
3. Shape dough into balls about 1 inch in diameter.
4. Beat egg white slightly and dip each ball into the egg white.
5. Roll in chopped walnuts.
6. Place on greased cookie sheet. Make fairly deep indentation in center of each cookie.
7. Bake at 350° F for 5 min. and then quickly indent the center a second time.
8. Bake for another 10 to 12 min. Remove from the oven and fill cookies with Pure Labrador Spread of your choice.

Steamed Partridgeberry Molasses Pudding

1 ½ cup	all purpose flour	375 ml
1 tsp	baking powder	5 ml
¼ tsp	salt	1 ml
½ cup	molasses	125 ml
1/3 cup	warm water	80 ml
2 tbsp	shortening melted	30 ml
2 tsp	soda	10 ml
2/3 cup	Pure Labrador Lingonberry (Partridgeberry) Spread	60 ml

1. Sift together flour, baking powder and salt.
2. Mix molasses, warm water, shortening and soda. Add to flour mixture.
3. Fold Pure Labrador Lingonberry (Partridgeberry) Spread into batter. Pour into a greased pudding mould. Cover tightly and place mould on a rack in the bottom of a deep saucepan. Add boiling water to half the depth of mould to the saucepan. Put lid on saucepan and steam for approximately two hours, checking frequently to ensure saucepan doesn't boil dry.

Serve hot with sauce.

Caramel Sauce:

1 cup	brown sugar	250 ml
1 ½ cup	boiling water	375 ml
Pinch	salt	Pinch
1 tbsp	custard powder	15 ml
2 tbsp	cold water	30 ml
2 tbsp	butter	30 ml
1 tsp	vanilla	5 ml

1. To make syrup: bring sugar, water and salt to a boil.
2. Mix custard powder with cold water. Add to syrup. Bring to a boil.
3. Add butter and vanilla. Keep warm

Dark Fruit Cake

Prepare pans: Grease well and line with greased waxed paper, two medium tube pans. Preheat oven to 275° F. Place a small ovenproof bowl or pan of water at the rear of centre oven rack.

¼ cup	all purpose flour, sifted	60 ml
1 lb	raisins	454 g
1 lb	currants	454 g
½ lb	dates	227 g
½ lb	orange peel	227 g
½ lb	citron chopped	227 g
½ lb	cherries cut in half	227 g
¾ cup	slivered almonds	185 ml
¾ cup	walnuts, chopped	185 ml
1 ½ cup	dark rum	325 ml
½ lb	butter	227 g
1 cup	brown sugar	250 ml
6	egg yolks, beaten until thick and lemon coloured	6
1 ¾ cups	all purpose flour, sifted	435 ml
1/8 tsp	baking soda	.5 ml
¾ tsp	mace	3 ml
¾ tsp	nutmeg	3 ml
1 ½ tsp	allspice	7 ml
½ tsp	cloves	2 ml
2 tsp	cinnamon	10 ml
½ tsp	ground ginger	2 ml
2 squares	unsweetened chocolate	2
½ cup	orange juice	125 ml
½ cup	molasses	125 ml
1 cup	strawberry jam	250 ml
6	egg whites, beaten until stiff but not dry	6

1. Lightly coat fruit in ¼ cup (60ml) flour and soak in 1 ½ cups dark rum overnight.
2. Cream very thoroughly butter and brown sugar. Add well beaten egg yolks. Combine dry ingredients. In top of double boiler, melt unsweetened chocolate; add orange juice, molasses and strawberry jam.
3. Add dry ingredients and liquids alternately to creamed mixture. Fold in fruit, almonds and walnuts blending well.
4. Fold egg whites into mixture.
5. Fill pans approximately two thirds full.
6. Bake in a slow oven 275° F for 3 to 4 hours, depending on oven but do not over bake.

Holidays & Times

Boiled Dark Fruit Cake
As told to us by Ruby Cabot.

Well I'll tell you now, it use to be in the month of November and things was scarce, so what mom use to do is she'd get a word to Aunt Mary Letemplier in Blanc Sablon and Aunt Mary would go around Hudson's Bay and she'd buy for her, the mixed peels and the mixed fruit and the raisins and the currents and cloves, stuff that she needed and dad would go up there, just before Christmas. Aunt Mary would give dad this package to bring back to mom. But dad didn't know what it was, because she was intending to make a few cakes now, and dad didn't like 'fer her to do that because it was giving away too much of his food.

But anyway, the cake she use to make was called the Boiled Dark Fruit Cake and this is the recipe for it. It was:

A half a pound of butter
Cup of sugar
Pack of raisins
Half pack mixed peels (4 oz pack)
Pack of currents
Cup of nuts
½ pound of dates
1 teaspoon of allspice
1 teaspoon of cinnamon
1 teaspoon of cloves
and 2 ½ cups of water.

And she'd boil that, all that mixture for fifteen minutes. And then she'd let it cool. And then after that she'd add in 3 teaspoons full of baking soda and she'd beat that well. Then she'd add in 3 cups of flour and flavoring. Flavoring would be vanilla. And then she'd bake the cake for approximately 2 ½ hours at 300 degrees.

What she'd do then, after she'd get her cakes made, she'd hide them away outside in the pantry in the cold and a day before Christmas. Now she'd send us around to all different people now, with our cakes. We was down to Aunt Theresa Cabot's, and down to Aunt Jane's, and over to Aunt Ri's, and over to Aunt Mag, but anyway it would go on.

But anyway that's what she'd give them all for Christmas. And that was a really good gift. And I tell you now, her cakes was good. Mom made them right up until, just before… about ten years before she died.

Aunt Pearl's Plate Cake
A heritage recipe as told to us by Lilly Fowler

Ingredients: 1 cup of butter , 1 cup of sugar , 3 eggs , 3 cups of flour , 3 teaspoons of baking powder , 1 ½ cup of raisins , 1 teaspoon of vanilla , ¾ cup of milk .

Mix all ingredients together. Place in a 9 x 13 inch dish, bake at 325° F for 45 to 50 minutes.

Great Grandmother's Gingerbread
A heritage recipe as told to us by Olive Marshall.

Ingredients:
½ cup of butter or lard
½ cup of sugar
1 egg (slightly beaten)
1 cup of molasses
2 ½ cups of sifted flour
1 ½ teaspoon of baking soda
½ teaspoon of salt
1 teaspoon of cinnamon
1 teaspoon of ginger
½ teaspoon of cloves
1 cup of hot water

Cream butter and sugar, add beaten egg and molasses. Mix well. Blend in [sifted] dry ingredients. Add hot water last and mix until smooth. Bake in a 9 inch square pan for 45 minutes at 350° F.

Steamed Molasses Pudding

Alma Goudie shared her recipe for steamed pudding with us. She would cook it when she had a jig's dinner and for Christmas she would serve it with a Hard Sauce.

Ingredients:
¼ cup shortening & ¼ cup of butter
1 beaten egg
¼ cup brown sugar
½ cup molasses

Beat well and then blend in ½ cup milk. Set aside.

Blend or stir together:
1 ½ cups flour
½ tsp baking soda
½ tsp salt
¾ tsp cinnamon
¼ tsp nutmeg

Add to liquid mixture and beat well. Fold in 1 cup of floured raisins, currants or chopped dates (or 1/3 of each of the three). Turn into a greased 1 quart mould. Cover and steam for 2 ½ hours.

Hard Sauce
(If Served as a Christmas Pudding)

¾ cup softened butter
2 cups sifted icing sugar
1 tsp vanilla
1 tsp rum
(Optional) ¼ cup coconut

Cream butter with the sugar until light and smooth.
Beat in vanilla and rum store, covered, in the refrigerator until serving time.

Cherry Cake

Prepare medium tube pan and preheat oven to 325° F. Place a small heatproof bowl of water on middle rack of oven at the rear. This will provide moisture while cake is baking.

1 ½ cups	butter	375 ml
2 cups	granulated white sugar	500 ml
3	eggs	3
3 ½ cups	all purpose flour	875 ml
1 ½ tsp	baking powder	7 ml
1 cup	milk	250 ml
½ cup	glace cherries, halved	125 ml
½ cup	maraschino cherries, halved	125 ml
1/3 cup	slivered almonds, toasted	80 ml
2 tbsp	lemon juice	30 ml

1. Cream butter and sugar until fluffy.
2. Add eggs, one at a time.
3. Blend flour with baking powder.
4. Add flour to creamed mixture alternately with milk.
5. Mix well and add cherries, almonds, and lemon juice.

Bake for 1 hour on middle rack of oven.
Note: Gum drops can be added instead of cherries.

Old Fashioned Christmas Sweet Bread

2	pkg yeast	2
1 cup	lukewarm water	250 ml
2 tsp	granulated white sugar	10 ml

1. Dissolve yeast in lukewarm water to which granulated sugar has been added. Whisk after 5 minutes.

12 cups	all purpose flour	3 L
6 tbsp	granulated sugar	90 ml
3 tsp	salt	15 ml
3 cups	raisins	750 ml
3 cups	lukewarm water	750 ml
1 cup	molasses	250 ml
3 tbsp	melted butter	45 ml

2. Sift together flour, granulated sugar, salt. Add raisins. Set aside.
3. Combine 3 cups lukewarm water, molasses and melted butter. Stir in dissolved yeast.
4. Add dry ingredients and raisins. Knead for 10 minutes.
5. Place in a greased bowl and turn dough over 2 or 3 times to grease the top and prevent a crust from forming. Cover and let rise until doubled, approximately 2 hours.
6. Knead dough and divide into 4 or 5 pieces. Form into loaves. Place in greased pans and let rise in warm area until doubled, approximately 1 hour.
7. Preheat oven to 325° F.
8. Bake until loaves give a hollow sound when tapped on the bottom, approximately 30 minutes.
9. Turn out of pans, brush with melted butter while hot.

Ethel's Oatmeal Chocolate Chip Cookies

Preheat oven to 350° F. Line cookie sheet with parchment paper.

¾ cup	butter	375 ml
1 ¼ cup	brown sugar	185 ml
1	egg	1
1 tsp	vanilla	5 ml
1 ¼ cup	all purpose flour	310 ml
¾ tsp	baking powder	3 ml
½ tsp	baking soda	2 ml
½ tsp	salt	2 ml
1 ¼ cup	quick cooking rolled oats	310 ml
½ cup	pecans, chopped	125 ml
½ cup	chocolate chips	125 ml

1. Cream butter and sugar.
2. Add egg and vanilla.
3. Combine flour, baking powder, baking soda and salt.
4. Add to creamed mixture.
5. Fold in oats, pecans, and chocolate chips
6. Roll into balls.   Flatten slightly.
7. Bake at 350° F for 10 minutes or until barely browned.

The Best Easy Chocolate Cake

Preheat oven to 350° F

1 ½ cups	all purpose flour	375 ml
1 cup	granulated white sugar	250 ml
½ tsp	baking soda	2 ml
¼ tsp	salt	1 ml
½ cup	cocoa powder	125 ml
2 oz	unsweetened dark chocolate, finely chopped	57 g
1 cup	hot coffee	250 ml
2/3 cup	mayonnaise	160 ml
1 large	egg	1
2 tsp	vanilla	10 ml

1. Whisk together flour, sugar, baking soda and salt in large bowl.
2. In separate bowl, combine cocoa powder and chocolate. Pour hot coffee over cocoa mixture and whisk until smooth, let cool slightly.
3. Whisk mayonnaise, egg and vanilla into cooled chocolate mixture.
4. Gently fold into dry ingredients. Mix until combined.
5. Pour into greased 8" x 8" pan.
6. Bake at 350° F for 20 to 35 minutes.

Index

Index

Notes

Notes